FINDING SACRED SECULAR IN THE

DONALD EARL PAULK

FOREWARD BY BISHOP EARL PAULK

**finding sacred
in the secular**

**Copyright 2000
Earl Paulk Ministries
Atlanta, Georgia**

**Printed in the United States of America
ISBN 0-917595-50-5**

FOREWORD

by Archbishop Earl P. Paulk

The average infant first learns to crawl, then to walk. Donald Earl Paulk wasted no time on either of these. At the age of seven months, he began to run. This natural example seems to be a pattern that has typified his spiritual life. It seems to me that even from his infancy he was being prepared to be a leader in the church for a new day.

When he responded to the call of God on his life, God seemed to mature him quickly. His call was not only to restore hurting people, but to respond to a "groaning earth" as well. At the age of 19, again he began to run.

Multi-cultural has never been a cliché to him. It is his life. His friends from childhood and in his adult life have been almost exclusively African-American. He never knew what it was to be surrounded only by people of similar culture. In his neighborhood, as a Caucasian, he was always the minority.

As I watch him and listen to him preach and lead worship in the Cathedral I am very much aware that God has prepared him to be a minister for the new millennium. He does not think old thoughts of "Church As Usual" (CAU). His mind is constantly developing new strategies to challenge world systems through **infiltration**.

I am convinced that his ears hear sounds that older ears can't hear. Revelation 14 speaks of a generation to come that will hear and sing a song that others were not able to hear or sing. He is not merely a survivor, but a revolutionary who embodies the **violent** spirit necessary to deride the strongholds of Satan. The Word of God tells us that Jesus is "held in the heavens" until this earth is made his footstool and until all authority and power is given back to God the Father. This authority can be reclaimed only when we decide to go into Satan's territory (world systems) and reclaim it.

This book is but a brief glimpse, from the mind of one of tomorrow's leaders, into the future. I am sure there will be many more to come! I urge you to read *Finding Sacred in the Secular* with intense interest because it speaks of how the church of tomorrow can be a viable force in society, not merely a barking dog chasing after the train of world systems. If the church is to survive as a force in the next millennium, it must listen to these new young prophetic voices!

ACKNOWLEDGMENTS

To my Archbishop, Earl P. Paulk, Jr. - My pastor, my uncle, my mentor, my spiritual father, my confidant, my friend. Thank you for the greatest gift that a father could give to a son, revelation. Everything in this book is an expression of the seed you have sown into my life.

To my Dad, Pastor Donald L. Paulk - You have labored and sown into a field that will not yield a harvest to you, but to your children. Your children will surely "rise up and call you blessed."

To my Mom, Clariece Paulk - I honor you for "pondering" in your heart the promises of God. You are my source of faith and hope.

To my wife, Brandin - I have followed the command to "seek" first the Kingdom of God and now I have the desires of my heart; I have you!

To my daughter, Esther - God has birthed you into His Kingdom for an "hour such as this." Learn all you can in the palace, but don't believe everything you learn. You are my joy.

To my sister, LaDonna Diaz - Thank you for the hours of laboring to birth my heart. Even though God has called you to be my scribe, you will always be my "sissy."

To Dana Harris - You are so much more to me than a cousin or even a brother, you are a co-laborer in the harvest.

To Deanna Maxwell - The spirit of Aunt Joan is alive. "Blessed are the peacemakers." Thank you for raising me!

To Randy Renfroe - As a child, my mother told me there are two kinds of people: givers and takers. You truly are a giver! Your calling makes it possible for me to hear from God.

To the editing staff - Pastor Don L. Paulk, Pastor Chad A. Hyatt, LaDonna Paulk Diaz, Teresa Martin and Charlotte Lemons - thank you for seeing the vision.

To the Presbytery and members of the Cathedral of the Holy Spirit - This book would not exist without your prayers and support.

I love you all!
DEP

**finding sacred
in the secular**

Contents

finding sacred in the secular

**finding sacred
in the secular**

**finding sacred
in the secular**

LOSING MY RELIGION

A Georgia based musical group named R.E.M. wrote a song called *Losing My Religion*. After expressing the deepest and most secret, hidden thoughts of his heart, the writer second guesses himself by saying, **"Oh no! I've said too much."** But then, a feeling of boldness comes over him, and in the next line he proclaims, **"I haven't said enough!"**

In the process of writing this book I have felt both of these emotions. I have felt fear and doubt because of the controversial nature of the material discussed (Oh no! I've said too much). Yet, I have also had a constant sense of certainty concerning this mission of God of mine to say things that are long overdue (I haven't said enough).

In this book you will hear two different voices talking to you. The first will come and tell you not to rock the boat. It will tell you that the shame and ridicule are not worth it. This voice will ask you questions like: "Doesn't it feel good to be liked?" "What will your family say?" "What will your friends say?" "What will your denomination say?"

But a second voice will speak to you and say, "Yes, this is the truth I have waited for." This voice will ask you to consider the cost and begin the journey. The second voice, unlike the first, will ask, "What if I don't do it?" "What will the world do?" "What will I think about myself?" More importantly this voice will ask, **"What will God think about me?"**

As you read this book, I would ask you to continually ask the Holy Spirit to allow you to read without prejudice: not racial prejudice, but a worse kind even than that - religious prejudice. The only way to understand this book is to completely deprogram your mind of all the religious tradition and trimmings that would keep your mind in a box.

Those who find comfort and solace in old ideas, even if the old ideas are wrong, do not readily accept new ideas. A belief system is something that gives most people security and stability. I have found that sometimes people would rather be wrong and secure, than right but in new and unfamiliar territory. Many of the doctrines people hold on to are not only lacking scriptural foundation, but are also not in keeping with the nature and character of Christ.

*I have found
that sometimes
people would
rather be wrong
and secure,
than right but in
new and
unfamiliar
territory.*

The first chapter of this book is somewhat of a test. It is similar to your freshman year in college. Remember that English professor whom you could have sworn was Satan himself in disguise? Would it surprise you to know that classes like these and professors like him are strategically placed purposely to try

4

and weed out those who are not serious about higher education?

This book is not for everybody. But before you put it down right now, perhaps I can offer some comfort to your mind by telling you that we will not enter any new territory in this book. We will only follow Christ into the places he frequented while here on this earth. However, for many Christians, this *will* be new territory!

**finding sacred
in the secular**

chapter one

LOSING MY RELIGION

Late one night on a hilltop called Gibeon, a young man sits enjoying the smell of the incense that burns before him. It is a perfect night; not too hot, not too cold. A feeling of peace settles over him; the kind of peace that comes only when you know you have been obedient, fulfilling to the best of your ability what God has required of you. He has often felt that peace when he has come here to offer sacrifices to God as he has done tonight. He can hear the music from the village below him, and it lulls him into an undisturbed, childlike sleep. In a dream the Lord appears to him and says, "Ask! What shall I give you?" Solomon does not ask for prosperity, longevity or even to be pictured on the cover of *Charisma Magazine*. He asks only for wisdom.

While praying one night I felt the presence   of the Lord in a way that I cannot describe. I heard a voice say to me, "Ask! What shall I give you?" I can accept no credit for my response because I was not prepared to answer and was unaware of what my reply would be. My words seemed to surpass my conscious mind, as I heard myself asking God to grant me the gift of *perspective*. That seems awfully vague and underdeveloped. Perspective on what? How the church can become more irrelevant in society? How we as Christians should be exempt from taxes because we are God's gift to this world? What?

The Great Awakening

At the time that I uttered these words I did not know how drastically my life would change. Before this night of asking God for " perspective" my life was fairly normal; easy; happy. I was not aware that a violent spirit would be birthed in me that would not allow my mind to rest.

I was not aware that a violent spirit would be birthed in me that would not allow my mind to rest.

I had no idea that I would never again be able to watch television without wondering how what I was viewing would effect the mind of every other viewer from different cultures and backgrounds. Specifically, I could no longer watch Christian programs without thinking, "How does the world and secular society view this?"

Before this great awakening, I had never really challenged my mind to think of much more than basketball, food and sex. I took for granted that everything Christian personalities said was fact, and I liked it this way because I did not have to do any "homework." I could just accept everything that I heard. But my mind began to systematically deprogram the traditional religious views to which I had fallen prey.

I began to look very closely at the life, character, nature and words of Jesus Christ. What I found was shocking! **He hated religious people.** Well, given the fact that He was sinless, hate is a strong term. Jesus Christ had an utter disgust for religious people. He used terms such as "children of Satan," "brood of vipers," "workers of iniquity," etc. He actually addressed the "religious" people of his day in this manner. On second thought, maybe hate is not a strong enough word! My mind embarked on a spiritual journey that would take me out of the four walls of the church and into a new and unfamiliar territory . . . the world.

My mind embarked on a spiritual journey that would take me out of the four walls of the church and into a new and unfamiliar territory .. the world.

My Journey

One of the first areas I began to examine was the world of music. I asked myself a very simple question, "What is the difference between sacred and secular music?" I grew up in church, and both my parents are worship leaders. I understand the ability of sacred music to touch the heart and to lift the spirit – making you feel closer to God, and giving you strength to face uncomfortable circumstances. But I had also felt comfort and had been "touched" by secular music. This was in direct contradiction to the general attitude of Christian leaders — that all secular musicians are idiots and cry-babies hoping to gain attention with their outlandish fashions and lifestyles; and that the purpose of all secular music is to lure the

What is the difference between sacred and secular music?

sheep away from the flock and to cause innocent young people, after hearing a song one time, to begin drinking goat's blood, drawing pentagrams on their school books and God forbid, playing their records backwards in order to receive secret messages from Satan!

I love sacred music. The great hymns of the faith contain the most sound doctrine you will ever hear. But the sad reality is that these songs are heard only by Christians and those few non-Christians who are brave enough to venture into a church. This music, no matter how wonderful its message and theology, will not be heard by those who need it most; the ones who will not enter a church because of their background, or those who have been hurt by the church and are disillusioned.

The major difference between sacred and secular music, with obvious exceptions, is the market they target. Sacred music, for the most part, is played in church and sold in Christian bookstores; places that are not major hang-out spots for most "sinners." Sacred music is sold on Christian labels carrying stereotypes that scare the world away. Sacred music is listened to largely by a Christian audience.

On the other hand, both Christians and non-believers listen to secular music. Secular music is readily accessible to those who would never enter a church.

If the mission of Christ is to reach and to save those who are lost, how can we call ourselves "Christ-like" when we are not in the markets where the lost people are?

We can no longer believe we are going to reach a dying world from a Christian bookstore containing only Christian music and Christian literature on Christian labels! The closest attempt you may find here is a Christian "alternative" band with a similar sound as secular, but with watered-down lyrics; not too preachy, but not too carnal either. The more music I listened to, the more I began to realize that what the Christian market was missing is what the world has had all along ... influence! Influence is an elusive quality that cannot be bought or achieved by following a formula. It is God-given. So I guess there truly is something sacred about the secular world.

Once this realization hit me, I was forced to look deeper - beyond outward appearances. I didn't just want to see the symptoms. I wanted to get to the root of the problem. I watched hours of MTV trying to understand the concerns and problems my generation was voicing.

And the Lord said, "To what shall I liken this generation, and what are they like? They are like children sitting in the marketplace and calling to one another, saying :

The more music I listened to the more I began to realize that what the Christian market was missing is what the world has had all along... influence!

*'We played the flute for you
And you did not dance;
We mourned to you,
And you did not weep.'"
(Luke 7:31,32)*

I heard these musicians asking hard questions about the realities of life and realized that they are the children sitting in the marketplace crying out to us, the church, for answers.

I heard lyrics like: **"God, sometimes you just don't come through," "What if God was one of us?" "So how can a man make rules, when yet he has no love?" "Yeah, we'd break bread and wine, if there was a church we could receive in"** (Tori Amos, Joan Osborne, Lenny Kravitz, U2 respectively).

I truly believe that these are the people Jesus would associate with if he were here now: people with questions, disillusioned and hurting.

I realized that I would never be able to reach these people and answer their questions if I was not willing to listen long enough to hear what questions were being asked. I truly believe that these are the people Jesus would associate with if he were here now: people with questions, disillusioned and hurting. When I was bold enough to stop judging and condemning, I was able to see with perspective.

Let's Give Them Something To
Talk About

Let's look, for a moment, at just exactly who Jesus chose to associate with, and who he chose to defend. The classic Bible story of the woman caught in the act of adultery begins with the Pharisees bringing her to Jesus saying, *"By our law this woman should be stoned."* Jesus replies, *"The one without sin may cast the first stone."* After this statement, he does a strange thing. He kneels down and begins to write in the sand. The Bible does not record exactly what he wrote. But it must have been so significant, so powerful, so relevant to the people who stood in accusation that when he finished and looked up - the only thing left to say was, *"Woman, where are your accusers?"* Needless to say there was an early dismissal of the **Anal Retentive Pharisee of the Month Club!**

Everyone is entitled to speculate about what he wrote in the sand. I do not believe it was some deeply theological word or phrase. I do not believe it was some profound verse from the Old Testament. The Jesus I have fallen in love with became this woman's defense attorney. As her attorney, I believe he brought to light hard, cold factual evidence against the prosecuting party with the words he wrote. I believe he began to write things like the names of the women (or men!)

with whom they had been "involved," and the amount of money some of them had wrongly taken from disadvantaged people.

As he methodically laid out this evidence, the Bible says the Pharisees began to dismiss themselves "one by one," perhaps as their own sin was uncovered and they were in essence stripped naked and discredited. A good attorney presents good evidence!

For those of you who don't know, back in 1997-98 our President, William Jefferson Clinton, found himself in a little hot water with the country over an alleged affair he had with a White House intern. After denying it initially, he eventually admitted to the affair, and apologetically took responsibility for his wrong-doing. His political opponents, along with the media, had a field day with this situation and proceeded to drag the nation through the whole year and a half debacle, providing us with much more information than we wanted or needed.

A man named Larry Flynt, who is the C.E.O. of a popular pornographic magazine called *Hustler*, came to the defense of the President. He, like many others in the nation, saw the absolute absurdity and hypocrisy of a situation in which men and women who, in many cases, were guilty of infidelity themselves, were standing daily in front of cameras hurling accusations and criticisms at the President for a personal failure which, in some people's opinion, had very little to do with his ability to run the country. Mr. Flynt made it known that he would issue a one million dollar reward to anyone who had legitimate proof of marital unfaithfulness on the part of any of the prosecuting attorneys or Senators or Congressmen who were part of the "Clinton bashing." He did indeed get his information, and more than one political figure ended up with egg on his face. Some resigned. Others just shut up, which is what they should have done in the first place. *Let him who is without sin cast the first stone...*

When I began to "lose my religion," I started asking questions like, "How is what Larry Flynt did for President Clinton any different than the biblical account of what Jesus did for the woman caught in the act of adultery?" In both cases the defendants were guilty. Both were caught "red handed." And in both cases, someone took it upon themselves to expose the hypocrisy and to say to those who had committed the sin, "Where are your accusers?"

I also began to ask a more important question: "Why has no renowned pastor come to the aid of our President?" While many preachers, some perhaps guilty of the same sin, cashed in on a chance for an extra "amen" or two at the President's expense, the founder and owner of a successful porn magazine was busy acting in the nature and character of Christ: defending him! Please don't misunderstand me and think

How is what Larry Flynt did for President Clinton any different than the biblical account of what Jesus did for the woman caught in the act of adultery?

that I condone how Larry Flynt makes his living, or his lifestyle. Actually, I don't know much about his lifestyle, so I am in no position to judge it. He may or may not profess to know Jesus Christ. All I know is that his actions in this case were more Christ-like than most preachers who fill pulpits every Sunday morning.

Whether you are a Democrat or a Republican; whether you think the President has done a good job or not is not the issue. The issue is that the church is called to restore, not to stone. Do you fall into the category of the Pharisees and self-righteous preachers who come to bring condemnation? Or do you gladly list yourself with the defenders of sinners: Jesus Christ - Larry Flynt?

Opium Anyone?

Religion is and has always been the *opiate* of the masses. We must leave the bondage of religion and dare to be spiritual. The gospels are very clear in their description of the Pharisees; they are the ones who "would not enter, or let anyone else enter" the Kingdom of God. They did not want to hear truth and did not want anyone else to hear it either.

We must leave the bondage of religion and dare to be spiritual.

Their sole purpose was to keep people under the bondage of religious law. Jesus Christ came to free us from the bondage of that law. The Pharisees mastered the law but they could not do one very important thing. They could not recognize that Jesus was the Son of God. The Pharisees could not see that Jesus was God in the flesh, dwelling among them. It was the sinner who called Him "Lord." It was the prostitute who called him "Master." It was the drunkard, the adulterer, the tax collector who recognized him as "Messiah."

It is impossible for the religious mind to comprehend the material that will be discussed in this book. At this point it is expedient that you ask the Holy Spirit for understanding. In order to derive any benefit from this book you must be willing to remove every prejudice from your mind.

In Galatians 6:1 Paul instructs the Galatians to be spiritual. *"Those who are spiritual, restore those who have fallen into temptation."* My prayer is that together we may leave the slavery of religiosity and begin the journey of becoming a spiritual people who really understand the concept that being a Christian is being like Christ.

It was the sinner who called him "Lord." It was the prostitute who called him "Master." It was the drunkard, the adulterer, the tax collector who recognized him as "Messiah."

finding sacred
in the secular

chapter two

FRIEND OF SINNERS

The "friend of sinners" was the derogative name the Pharisees called Jesus. If you take the time to read the gospels you will find that each of them has a different perspective on the events surrounding the life of Jesus because they were written by four different people with four different perspectives and styles of writing. In these four different accounts, however, one fact remains the same; Jesus was a friend to the sinner.

It is commonly known that Mary Magdalene was a prostitute or at least a "woman in the city who was a sinner." We also know that she became one of Jesus' closest friends and financial supporters. Many can accept this only because they believe that after her first encounter with Jesus she totally changed her lifestyle. But have you ever considered that this may not be the case?

If you look closely at the travels of Christ in his ministry you will see that he often ministered in Bethany. Bethany was called the "house of misery" because of all of the invalids who gathered there. While in Bethany, ministering to the outcasts, he usually stayed with his good friend Lazarus. Many theologians speculate that Mary Magdalene was the sister of

Lazarus because the Bible, in several different accounts, speaks of Mary Magdalene in very similar phrases and stories as it speaks of the woman known as Mary of Bethany.

Would this mean that Jesus stayed at the same house where Mary Magdalene ran her business of prostitution? What if he did? Maybe she had changed her lifestyle. But what if she hadn't? Would Jesus have still chosen to stay in a house where prostitution and sinful deeds were taking place? Would he have loved these friends of his any less or treated them any differently? It's a question worth thinking about.

Let us rehearse what many of you are now trying to skip over. First of all, Jesus chose to minister in Bethany, the place where the invalids chose to congregate. Secondly, he chose to stay in a present or past house of prostitution during his ministry in Bethany. Next, Jesus distinguished Mary by calling her "Magdalene" (a strong tower or fortress). And finally, he allows Mary Magdalene to financially support his ministry with money she earned from prostitution. Now is the time to pour yourself a glass of water and swallow this jagged little pill called reality. Jesus was a friend of sinners.

Proud Mary

Mary Magdalene is seen washing Jesus' feet with very expensive fragrant oil that she has prepared for his burial (another reference showing the likelihood of Mary of Bethany and Mary Magdalene being the same person). As the tears run down her face and drip off of her chin onto his feet, she takes her hair and dries them away.

This intimate display causes some to be so scared that someone will think Mary had inappropriate feelings for Jesus that their focus is taken off of her complete gratitude and thankfulness. For instance, Judas allows his focus to be taken off of an incredible display of love, affection and forgiveness. Interestingly, his concern is on how much the fragrance could have been sold for.

What they all fail to see is that Mary's ability to wash Jesus' feet with her hair came from the same place that caused Jesus to call her a tower and a fortress. Mary Magdalene, a tower and a fortress? Yes. Her power to be that tower and fortress lay in her ability to recognize that she was sinful and that she had been forgiven freely by a man who was so confident in his calling and purpose that he slept in her house while she was still in sin.

Would history record the story of Mary Magdalene if Christ had not reached out to her in her most sinful state? Obviously Jesus saw past the symptoms she was exhibiting and got to the root of her problem, a lack of love and low self-esteem. He saw past all that and loved her anyway – probably something that no one had done for her before.

'Cause I'm The Tax Man

My sister is the children's minister at our church and she is in the process of writing a curriculum for the children because so much of the material written for this age is so vague and opinionated that those who know Jesus have a hard time teaching it. I asked her recently to sing to me a song I remember from child-hood about Zaccheus. So she sang:

"Zaccheus was a wee little man,
A wee little man was he.
He climbed up in a sycamore tree,
For the Lord he wanted to see.
As the Savior passed that way,
He looked up in the tree and said,
"Zaccheus, come down from there,
For I am going to your house today."

It is amazing to me that the part of this song children, and adults for that matter, remember most is that some really short guy climbed up into a tree to see Jesus. We fail to get the point of this song – the main issue – which is that Jesus went to eat at the home of a hated tax collector.

The Pharisees stand outside of Zaccheus' house (too afraid of how it would effect their reputations to enter themselves) asking Jesus' disciples how he can eat with such sinners. It interests me that they do not direct their question to Jesus. Even so, he is so eager to discredit them that when he overhears them he turns and answers them saying, *"The well have no need of a physician."*

Family Secrets

Many times when reading certain books of the Bible, all we seem to see are endless verses such as: Abraham begot Isaac, Isaac begot Jacob, Jacob begot Judah, etc. We become very bored and think that all of this was probably a lot more fun to those actually doing the "begetting" than to those of us who are plagued with having to read about it.

However, in the genealogy of Christ lay some very interesting facts. Judah, the son of Jacob had twin boys by Tamar who were named Perez and Zerah. Read Genesis 38:1-30 and you will see that Tamar is a harlot and that Perez and Zerah are conceived out of harlotry and incest. It is interesting to note that Judah had other children (Er, Onan, Shelah), but they are not mentioned in the genealogy of Jesus.

Furthermore, the Bible goes on to say how Judah, a man who has had children with his dead son's harlot wife, was to be obeyed by all God's people. The house of Zerah, the son of Tamar the harlot, is later referred to as a "blessed house." Do you mean to tell me that these people are in the ancestry and genealogy of the Son of God? And you thought your family tree had a few bad apples!

Oh, I forgot to mention that Rahab, who appears five generations after Tamar, is a harlot as well. You remember Rahab – she's the one who delivered Joshua out of the hand of the king of Jericho. Hebrews 11:31 even says, *"By faith, the harlot Rahab did not perish with those who did not believe."* Hold on one minute! Are you telling me that there are two harlots or prostitutes listed in the genealogy of Jesus Christ? Yes, not to mention David, Bathsheba, Manasseh and many other well-known Bible characters whose actions often bordered on the maniacal.

*You may think
that I am going
to great
lengths to
associate
Jesus with
harlots,
drunkards, tax
collectors and
sinners.
There's a good
reason for that
- I am!*

You may think that I am going to great lengths to associate Jesus with harlots, drunkards, tax collectors and sinners. There's a good reason for that – I am! Every person in Jesus' lineage was not perfectly

24

pure and holy. It is a fact that sin was present in the lives of some of his forbears. Jesus chose to be friends with people who were sinners, which says to me that he was not afraid of sin or of sinful people.

What Would Jesus Do?

The phrase "being Christ-like" should now take on a deeper meaning to you. You should ask yourself, "Do I have any friends who are sinners?" If your answer is no, the next question to yourself should be, "Why not?" Your reply may be, "I'm just not in the same environments they are." Then perhaps you are not as much like Christ as you think.

It is understandable that a recovering alcoholic should probably not be "hanging out" in bars trying to save others. It does take a certain amount of experience, strength and maturity to go to certain places and not be influenced by your surroundings. That is why you send soldiers to battle and not children!

A mature Christian can go into any environment, politics, education, entertainment, etc., and blend in without being overwhelmed by the negative influences. More importantly, a mature Christian can create relationships in these places without being "pushy" and

*Ironically,
many people
who wear the
"W. W. J. D."
(What would
Jesus do?)
bracelets
know very
little about
what Jesus
would actually
do if He were
here.*

repulsive to those around them; and they most certainly won't condemn them.

Ironically, many people who wear the "W.W.J.D." (What Would Jesus Do?) bracelets know very little about what Jesus would actually do if he were here. I challenge you to ask someone wearing one of these bracelets how many unsaved friends they have. Jesus is not to be remembered as sinful, but he is to be remembered as being the "friend of sinners." Maybe someday I will be lucky enough to have a nickname like that!

chapter three

PENDULUM SWING

I recently told someone that my biggest fear in life is not that a Christian will see me with a prostitute, an alcoholic or drug addict, or even with a homosexual. My biggest fear is for someone in the world, who has never been properly shown the grace, love and acceptance of God, to see me with a self-righteous, judgmental, condemning Christian. If they did, they might stereotype me as that kind of person as well, and destroy any chance I may have to reach them. Being seen with sinful people only places me in the company of Jesus Christ.

Being seen with sinful people only places me in the company of Jesus Christ.

We see many times the differences between generations. For example, my mother's mother was a "neat freak", and was very strict in her disciplining of my mother and her siblings concerning the physical condition of their home. My mother had to make her bed every morning and not sit on it again until it was time to go to sleep.

For this reason my mother "swung" to the other extreme and did not demand very much from me or my sister concerning the maintenance of a spotless house. After all, why make your bed when you are just going to sleep in it and mess it up again?

My father was not quite as unconcerned about messy rooms and used to post notes on my bedroom door that read like this: "Anyone entering this bedroom may do so only if he is current on all of his shots, especially his tetanus shot." One time my sister had so many clothes on her floor that you could not see what color the carpet was. After several requests for her to clean up a little, my father piled her clothes into a trash bag and hid them in our attic. He told LaDonna that he had thrown them away because she obviously didn't think enough of them to take care of them properly, and that she would just have to find something else to wear. After some serious pouting, she began to search for something to wear to church. When she couldn't find anything, and Dad was convinced she had learned her lesson, he returned her clothes to her. As far as cleaning was concerned, he didn't swing as far to the extreme as my mother because, although his parents were hard on him in other areas, housekeeping had not been a major issue in his house.

Stuck In The Middle With You

When the pendulum swings from one extreme to the other between generations, we seem only to go around the mountain one more time, making no more progress than the generation before us did.

When the pendulum swings from one extreme to the other between generations, we seem only to go around the mountain one more time, making no more progress than the generation before us did. Hopefully, I will learn from this, and not be an irrational dictator with my children just because my parents were much less strict on me than their parents were on them. Probably, the healthiest place for a parent to be is somewhere between the "neat freak/ dictator/ disciplinarian" and the "permissive slob." (Disclaimer: Mother, I am not calling you a permissive slob.) Health and truth are usually found in tension, the place in the middle of two extremes. Unfortunately, some Christians never apply this truth to their daily walk.

Many newborn Christians come from a background of addiction, abuse, lawlessness and sin. When they come to Christ they must experience a time of "separation" or "sanctification" from these former things that once controlled and enslaved them. During this time of "separation" they should be nurtured and discipled in the Word of God.

This time of separation should be a time for them to gain strength and wisdom. However, there is also a time when that person must go back to the places and to the people they were once involved with to show how the grace of God can restore their lives as well. But many converts never return to those places and people because they are afraid of also returning to that old lifestlye. They feel they have suddenly gained a reputation that will not allow them to be seen with those who are not "saved." The very heart of the Christian message is to share the gospel we have heard and received with others. I am baffled by how few really understand this and am saddened by those

pendulum swing

Health and truth are usually found in tension, the place in the middle of the two extremes. Unfortunately, some Christians never apply this truth to their daily walk.

who approach their old friends and associates with an "I'm better than you now"—snobbish, condescending attitude.

You're Not Happy – You Only Think You Are

Many conversations between new Christians and non-Christians begin with, "Don't you want to be happy?" When the non-Christian replies, "But, I am happy," the over-zealous new believer shakes his head with a knowing look on his face and says, "No, you're not happy. You only think you are." Will somebody please tell me the difference between being happy and thinking you are happy? Aren't you happy if you think you are? This approach makes no sense to me, and guess what? It makes no sense to non-Christians either. It serves only to confirm their suspicions that Christianity is a cult that sucks the intelligence and free will right out of you.

Christians make a mistake when they begin a relationship with a non-Christian with this attitude: "Watch me and listen to what I say, and you will see how Jesus can change your life too." The proper approach to a person who does not know Christ does not have the word change anywhere near it. It is not the Christian's job to change others. Our job is to let them know by our actions as well as by our words that salvation is a free gift of grace Jesus offers to us. Change will come, but it is made more unlikely by a person who emphasizes it too strongly or too soon in a relationship with a non-Christian. True freedom and change come when people are set free from the bondage of the law and allow Christ's finished work to take over in their lives.

If I Built This Fortress Around Your Heart

Many times God calls people into the ministry who have very sinful backgrounds. After their conversion or "new birth" they suddenly begin to build within their hearts a fortress of hatred for sin and for the consequences associated with it. The catastrophe of this is that they also seem to suddenly become intolerant of sinners. With their newly acquired "zeal," they dig an incredibly deep and uncrossable chasm between themselves and the world; the same world that Jesus loves and died for.

I have observed that it is usually the men or women who were once considered, at least in their own minds, extremely sinful who become the most ignorant, irrelevant, condemning, fiery, "fire and brimstone" preachers. These preachers never realize that they are quickly disqualifying themselves from ever truly reaching the lost. I challenge you to watch their lives and ministries closely. They are often the very ones who become overwhelmed by temptation and fall prey to

pendulum swing

It is not the Christian's job to change others. Our job is to let them know by our actions as well as by our words that salvation is a free gift of grace Jesus offers to us.

31

sexual affairs and scandals or secretly become addicted to alcohol, drugs or pornography. Why? Because their sinful passions will continue to be aroused by the law as long as they live under it and try to force others to do so as well (Romans 7:5,6).

Falling From Grace

It is important now to clarify what grace really is. We hear more and more frequently about preachers "falling from grace." Many Christians who have what I call the "inquiring-mind" syndrome equate someone's falling from grace with sins of the flesh, and they cannot wait to read every little, nasty detail. They fail to realize that it is impossible for us to fall from grace back into sin, because we were never sinless to begin with. We have been taken out from under the law that once oppressed us, and have been placed under a new and even higher law: the law of grace. Still, we will always be sinful! If not, there would be no need for grace.

...it is impossible for us to fall from grace back into sin, because we were never sinless to begin with.

Falling from grace, then, actually means the opposite of what most people believe it means. The only way that anyone, clergy or lay person, can "fall from grace" is not to fall into sin, but to fall back into the law. Paul wisely tells is in Galatians 5, *"You have become estranged from Christ, you have attempted to be justified by law; you have fallen from grace."* I suppose some of us are just destined to be like the "foolish Galatians," entering into the new birth through faith in Christ, but then turning right around to the law again for justification (Galatians 3:1-3).

When we do this we become like the dog that returns to its vomit. Even more disgusting and sickening, we cause the death of Christ to be in vain. *"I do not set aside the grace of God; for if righteousness comes through the law, then Christ died in vain," Galatians 2:21.*

Ignorantly, many pastors stuff the "law" down the throats of new Christians as if it is to be a staple in their diet, which usually serves only to ensure they will have more sin in their lives, thus creating more consequences. In Romans 7:5-6, Paul says, *"For when we were in the flesh, the sinful passions which were aroused by the law were at work in our members to bear fruit to death. But now we have been delivered from the law, having died to what we were held by, so that we should serve in the newness of the Spirit and not in the oldness of the letter."*

Ultimate Freedom

The truth that has been revealed to me is that ultimate freedom can be experienced only when we are no longer held in bondage by the law. Without the constant pressure of fulfilling the law, your mind is

Without the constant pressure of fulfilling the law, your mind is free to use all of its energy and creativity fulfilling your God-given purpose and destiny.

free to use all of its energy and creativity fulfilling your God-given purpose and destiny. Strangely enough, I have found in my own life that my tendency toward temptation and sin has drastically decreased now that my sinful passion is no longer being aroused by my attempts to follow the letter of the law!

After we are born again we will still constantly sin and make mistakes. Romans 3:23 says, *"For all have sinned and fall short of the glory of God."* This verse has incorrectly been preached, for all have sinned and have fallen short... Fallen is not the tense of the word that is used. The tense is present: fall. This form of the word functions not only as its present tense, but also as its future tense.

For example, when teaching young children about tenses a simple sentence structure relating to different times is often used: "I fall today," "I fell yesterday," "I have fallen many times before." For future tense it would be taught, "I may fall tomorrow." I think this same method should be adopted when teaching young Christians about sin, except instead of using "may," use this phrase: "I will definitely fall tomorrow." The Amplified Bible reads, *"Since all have sinned and are falling short..."* We must realize that even after salvation we will continue to sin and to fall, but the important thing is that through the grace Christ offers us we can get back up and still fulfill our purpose for God's Kingdom. That purpose is for our lives to become a living testimony for us to share with those whom it may benefit. The only way that "all things can truly work together for our good" is for us to let our past, present and future failures serve to help someone else.

When we have gone through situations, struggles and temptations that are similar to another person's plight, but because of pride or fear, will not be a friend to them during their crisis, we are not being Christ-like. In the Old Testament, the high priests did not have much personal contact with the people who were not part of the Levitical Order. The lives they led were so structured with rules and regulations that I'm sure they didn't have the time to commit many fleshly sins. Because of this it was extremely difficult for them to empathize with the common man because they literally had not had many opportunities to share like experiences with them. It is understandable in this regard that they had very little compassion.

But then God sent his own son, and purposely let him feel everything that his fellowman felt. The Bible describes him as a high priest who is touched with the feelings of our infirmities, which was a completely new concept at that time. When the infirmities of others no longer touch us and stir within us Christ-like compassion, we lose our ability to be of any help to the lost as we become more ineffective than the high priests

The only way that "all things can truly work together for our good" is for us to let our past, present and future failures serve to help someone else.

of old. At least they had some reason to act as they did. How dare we who have experienced the consequences of sin deny that fact and act as if we are now too good to stoop to the sinner's level.

Do No Harm

When a medical student becomes a doctor, he or she takes what is called The Hippocratic Oath. As a part of this, the doctor must promise to do no harm to a patient. This basically means that if he reaches a point where he can do no more good - he cannot heal – then he, at least, should not make the situation any worse. He should do no harm.

The goal of both the doctor and the pastor is to save lives. And saving lives cannot always be done in a completely sterile environment.

The goal of both the doctor and the pastor is to save lives. And saving lives cannot always be done in a completely sterile environment. It is fairly obvious that the environment of an elective surgery operating room and that of an emergency room are different. In the case of elective surgery there is time to take every precaution. But as most of us know from watching E.R. on television, time is not always unlimited in emergency situations. When someone's life is at stake, the doctors and nurses do the best they can to provide a sterile, clean environment, but if it comes down to it, they just have to leave that dirty work shirt on the construction worker while they fight to save his half-severed leg.

And what happens when a doctor is faced with having to handle a life-threatening situation away from an emergency room? What if no sterile gloves are available? I guarantee you that any doctor worthy of his profession would still do whatever he could to save that life, gloves or no gloves – even at the risk of infecting himself.

Our fear-driven attempts at reaching the world wearing sterile gloves must cease. Those who are afraid of contracting a disease from a sinful world will never reap the harvest. Only those who are willing to remove their sterile gloves and get a little dirt under their fingernails will be effective. Yes, the harvest is ripe, but the field that we work in and plant in is full of dirt.

Our fear-driven attempts at reaching the world wearing sterile gloves must cease.

We must be willing to sacrifice that reputation we think we have a right to, and as Paul said in I Corinthians 9:19-23, *"become all things to all men."* Let us fight with everything in us to stop that pendulum midway in its swing so that it never again reaches the extremism that causes us to see the world through religious glasses. Let us truly see the world and the people in the world as Christ sees them. By taking on his mind, we can and must lose our religion in order to reach a hurting and dying world.

PART TWO

NO TRESPASSING

chapter four
GREEN PASTURES

chapter five
SIGHT BEYOND SIGHT

chapter six
NO TRESPASSING

finding sacred
in the secular

GREEN PASTURES

The phrase "green pastures" calls to mind for most of us a picture of the good shepherd leading us through a peaceful, grassy field, our hair gently blowing in the wind. Deer can be spotted through the trees in the distance as children fly kites and play nicely with each other. A woman wearing a sun dress and straw hat is sitting at the edge of a babbling brook, occasionally throwing a rock in or putting her feet in the water. A serene and tranquil setting if ever there was one. But, if you will be so patient and kind as to humor me, I will attempt to offer you an alternate perspective of the green pasture spoken of in the 23rd Psalm.

The greenest pasture is one that has never been walked upon. A true green pasture does not bear the evidence of a path. A path is visible only after people or animals have walked across it many times and have beaten away all that was once green. A green pasture is not a popular place where a multitude of people have chosen to congregate. It is new territory; a place where no one has never been before; and getting there is an adventure. The type of green pasture I want to describe to you is not an obvious place to most people. There are no hoof prints. It is not the brown, muddy place where the cows wait to be fed. It is *green*.

The greenest pasture is one that has never been walked upon. A true green pasture does not bear the evidence of a path.

If you have ever been around livestock you know that the muddiest place in the pasture is around the feeding trough. Animals fed from these troughs are not dissimilar to many Christians who come to church week after week only to be fed, or to get their "blessing," or to get their "shout on," or even better to give an offering once or twice a year that they expect miraculously to get them out of the debt they have accumulated from years of charging their credit cards to the limit, years of bad money management, and years of making bad decisions like marrying a man who is "employmentally challenged" ("unemployed" for those of you who are not afraid to be politically incorrect).

As the cows continue to congregate where they think they will be fed, they create a sloppy mud hole. They are unaware that the feeding time they enjoy so much every day serves only to fatten them up in preparation for their final destination – the slaughterhouse. They are ignorant of the fact that everything necessary to sustain them can be found out in the field: grass, wheat, grain, water, etc. But it is more *convenient* to just hang around the trough and wait to be fed.

Cows have never been accused of being the smartest animals on the planet. Neither have sheep, or for that matter, most animals who graze. These animals are not self-sufficient. They need a shepherd or a farmer to guide their very existence. That is why green pastures are never found by the flock. Green pastures are found by shepherds who must lead their flocks there.

To Boldly Go Where
No Man Has Gone Before

Only a genuine leader or shepherd who has the best interest of his sheep (or cows) at the forefront of his heart is willing to receive the ridicule, shame, and sometimes excommunication that entering new territory brings with it. And, of course, by now you should understand that I am using this metaphor to describe what happens in the church, the shepherd being the pastor, the animals the people, and the green pasture whatever new area in world systems God wants his church to influence for His kingdom.

Just what are these green pastures I keep alluding to? The best examples I can give you come from the ministry I know best. It is the ministry my uncle and father founded almost forty years ago now, and is where I have grown up. Over the years, our church has become known for entering into new territory in many areas. We began letting teenage girls perform interpretive dances on stage back when any form of organized dancing in the church was unheard of. But it really touched our people and brought something out in them that nothing else did, and there was scriptural basis for it. Dance became such a big part of our worhip that we began dance classes of all kinds and a dance company was actually formed under a minister of dance. Now it is quite common to go into almost any charismatic church and see women in ballet slippers dancing down the aisles with banners, or even performing worshipful dances on the stage as part of a dance ministry. But back when we started it, in the late sixties and early seventies, we were highly criticized.

Rock And Roll Hoochie-Coo

At the end of the seventies we began having a weekly youth service at our church that featured a rock-n-roll band. The lyrics were all Christian, but the style of music was what most of the teenagers listened to daily on rock radio stations. From 1978 until 1987 this ministry grew from 35 kids meeting in the fellowship hall to over 2,500 teens packing out our main sanctuary. We called it Alpha, the beginning of new life through Jesus Christ.

Coming to church became "cool," and being saved wasn't just for nerds who had nothing else to do on the weekends.

It was indeed a move of God. Even though the band was nowhere near the level of the professional rock musicians of that era, this sound was new to the church, and something the kids of that generation could relate to. Because of this, it worked. Coming to church became "cool," and being saved wasn't just for nerds who had nothing else to do on the weekends. Jocks and cheerleaders, "heads" and "freaks," as the drug-users were called, came from high schools all over the Atlanta area.

When they got here it was dark, with colored lights shining only on the stage. The music was loud. Many of the people in the audience were good looking and popular. What teenager wouldn't want to come? But at the end of the night, the lights came up, and an invitation for salvation was given. This invitation never failed to bring teenagers flooding down to the front, often in tears where they were greeted, hugged, prayed for and accepted by others just like them, their lives changed forever.

We thought it was wonderful, yet we were scandalized by other local ministries for allowing the "devil's music" into our church. We were written up in the newspaper. We were accused of being a cult, all because we had dared to bring a set of drums and electric guitars into the church. It was a green pasture back then. Today this format of reaching teens is outdated in most large cities, but those churches who waited for it to become *kosher* are just now trying to begin ministries of this nature. They missed the boat. Yet they are still hanging on, vainly preparing for the "big revival" that is now highly improbable.

The church and religious minds have always seemed to think that if something is new and non-traditional, it

The Church and religious minds have always seemed to think that if something is new and non-traditional, it must be heretical.

45

must be heretical. But miraculously, five years after this new strategy is no longer attractive to the people in the world who we are called to reach; now that it has been out of style for several years and technology and trends have changed, the church somehow thinks enough time has passed for the practice to have become acceptable, and its heretical nature has suddenly vanished. *Now* they try it! And because they did not seize the day of its effectiveness; because they waited until the wave had crested and ebbed back into the ocean of pop culture, the number of souls that could possibly have been effected by it is very limited. All because they were too afraid to take the heat for trying something new. Fear destroys the possibility of reaping a bountiful harvest.

True spiritual pioneers feel so honored to have been shown this new territory that they walk very carefully, and teach those who follow them to do the same so that the pasture is not corrupted.

If You Can't Stand The Heat . . .

Finding green pastures and leading your flock there comes at a high price sometimes. True spiritual pioneers feel so honored to have been shown this new territory that they walk very carefully, and teach those who follow them to do the same so that the pasture is not corrupted. Unfortunately, once the dust has settled and the rest of the church world no longer equates this new strategy with heresy, the mercenary ministries (Micah 3:11) come in and endeavor to devise a marketing plan for this newly acceptable practice.

The larger flock now invades the new territory with all of their religiosity and selfish motives; and before you know it, the once green pasture has been trampled and stampeded into a muddy hole because no one has taken the time to teach them to walk carefully like the original shepherd did.

I believe there are many green pastures God desperately desires for his flock, but he knows that his shepherds are not ready for the exploration of new territory. Many of them are still too concerned with their own popularity, acceptance and reputation. He also knows that his sheep are not yet mature enough to walk carefully. They still enter into world systems boldly proclaiming their presence as "demon-stomping," "spirit-filled," "sin-hating Christians."

Where Have All the Cowboys Gone?

Where are the Abraham's? Where are the Joshua's and Caleb's? Where are the men and women who have heard from God and are willing to leave the comforts of their land – their feeding trough - and travel to *a land that they know not of,* killing giants if necessary?

I believe God is beginning to release a sound to be heard by his called and appointed shepherds. But as the sound reaches the ears of some of the shepherds their "mind of reason" comes alive. "What will my denomination think about this? If they cut me and my church off, where will we go? What will we eat? If we leave the feeding trough, we'll go hungry." I'm sure Moses had similar fears when God told him to take his people out of Egypt. But they were just fine. God provided food, clothing and shelter for them in the middle of a desert for forty years. If only shepherds could understand that when God truly gives a vision to someone, he is faithful to his word and will supply the provisions necessary to complete the assignment.

You may be asking at this point, "What's wrong with wanting to be responsible over those God has placed in your care? Didn't Jesus instruct his disciples to *feed my sheep*?" Yes, shepherds are responsible for feeding the flock, but for many, this is their only interest. They do not encourage their sheep to go out into the world and share with the people they find there the knowledge of God's love that they have been so freely given. *"Freely you have received, freely give!"* With a dying world to save, we cannot afford to grow comfortable in an "us four and no more" posture within our churches. Shepherds must constantly be in the process of reaching out to the lost and must teach their people to do so as well.

'Cause I've Been Through The Desert On A Horse With No Name

We have already discussed the characteristics of pastures where livestock graze, but to change paradigms for a moment, let us explore the idea that a "green pasture" does not necessarily have to be a place where grass grows. Consider our premise that a green pasture is new territory. A green pasture could be a wilderness or a desert place. Isaiah 40:3 says, *"Prepare in the wilderness the way of the Lord; make straight and smooth in the desert a highway for our God!"*

This verse has been taken out of context so many times. It has been preached to mean, "Rid your life of sin so that you can stay on the right path." The road that leads to God has been presented as a straight and narrow path, hard for the common sinner to travel down. As is made obvious by this erroneous interpretation of scripture, inexperienced, uneducated preachers who feel they are called into the ministry Saturday night at prayer meeting and begin preaching from the pulpit the next morning are extremely dangerous, and often do more harm than good by confusing people.

49

*The "green-
est" pastures
of our day are
indeed the
desert and
wilderness
places where
people of the
world are held
in bondage by
circum-
stances, but
are afraid to
walk into a
church be-
cause of the
stereotypes of
condemnation
and "brow-
beating" that
we have
created for
ourselves.*

Sometimes it is necessary to consult and study the original languages of Hebrew (Old Testament) or Greek (New Testament) to truly understand the meaning of the scriptures. In Greek, the wording of this verse literally means to *"clear away all the obstacles"* for God to be able to go into wilderness places, or in other words, make his path *"easily accessible"* to those who have found themselves in a wilderness place in life. The last part of the verse literally means to create a *"wide, level and passable"* path for God to be able to go into desert places. If we as Christians continually hang around the feeding trough, we will never go into places of desolation as Christ's ambassadors, creating avenues for him to work through.

The "greenest" pastures of our day are indeed the desert and wilderness places where people of the world are held in bondage by circumstances, but are afraid to walk into a church because of the stereotypes of condemnation and "brow beating" that we have created for ourselves. I cannot say that I blame them.

Consider the body of Christ from the world's point of view. They see how we treat our own when they fall into a pit. We ridicule, judge, distance ourselves and revoke licenses. Sometimes we even refuse phone calls from close friends in the ministry who are struggling for survival. Why should people in the world, who are seeking shelter and restoration, think that we would treat them any better than they see us treating our own supposed brothers and sisters?

If we truly desire to prepare the way for our Lord to return we can no longer simply pray for Babylon to fall and wait for the moon to turn to blood. Christ's return is not limited to a few chronological occurrences of natural disasters (earthquakes, floods, etc). It is dependent upon his church, his bride, being mature enough to be a comparable mate to him. As his bride, we must clear away all the obstacles that hinder people from receiving his grace. We must begin now to prepare a highway for him to go into the wilderness of secular places through *us*. Christ in us, *in the world*, is the hope of glory!

We must begin now to prepare a highway for Him to go into the wilderness of secular places through us.

Many green pastures lie before us today – government, science, medicine, education, law, business, the music industry, the film industry, television, the arts, etc. - but unless we pray for perspective, we will never truly see them, and will risk missing opportunities God is giving us to gain influence in these areas.

Teach Your Children Well

My father has told me a story many times about his father telling him, "Son, I would rather you be a preacher for God than to be the President of the United States of America." My father repeated these words to me after I responded to the call of God on my life at age 19, sacrificing a four year scholarship to play basketball at a Division I university. At the time, this story and my father's words gave me great comfort and solace, and I do believe I made the right choice. But the right choice for me is not necessarily the right choice for my children.

Truly serving God happens outside the church. Worshipping God is what happens inside the church.

I am now the father of a beautiful little girl and plan to have more children. I truly want, more than anything in my life, for my children to serve God. However, I do not believe the only way for them to serve God is from inside the four walls of the church. Truly serving God happens *outside* the church. Worshiping God is what happens *inside* the church. I hope one of them does become President of the United States. I wish that they would train themselves to become lawyers and legislators. I would be a happy and fulfilled father if my children were actors or great musicians in the secular world. Why?

A preacher in a church building, even one on a Christian television network, can reach only a limited group of people. He reaches only those who will enter his or her church or those who might happen across his or her television broadcast and be able to watch it long enough, without being turned off, to hear the good news of Christ. But a President, a legislator, an actor or famous musician all have the capability to reach millions of people who would very likely never associate themselves with the church.

As we embark on our journey, it is extremely important for us not to initiate a stampede that would destroy the green pasture with our religious tradition and bondage, and lessen our chance to make any real difference in that environment by vehemently proclaiming, "We are the children of God and we have come to change the lifestyle of everyone here!" Only when we learn how to properly maneuver in these new territories, will our influence for the Kingdom of God be limitless!

finding sacred
in the secular

5

SIGHT BEYOND SIGHT

I believe that a key ingredient to gaining influence in these new territories is our ability to see beyond what the average Christian sees. We find that Jesus has this ability in the story found in Matthew 9:35-38. He is overwhelmed with compassion for a mass of lost and helpless people who are following him. Immediately he says to his disciples, *"The harvest truly is plentiful, but the laborers are few."* Why does Christ equate these lost and wandering vagabonds to a plentiful harvest?

This contradiction in thought only leads me to assume that he saw something more than a bewildered group of sinful people. Jesus saw the possibility of what these people could become. Next, he gives the command for his disciples to pray that laborers would be sent out to reap this harvest of people. The amplified Bible says, *"So pray to the Lord of the harvest to force out and thrust laborers into his harvest."* Christ had *sight beyond sight* to see through the problems and the sin of the amassed people. He saw a harvest of souls! How can we gain this seemingly supernatural quality of sight? I think the answer lies in our ability to understand the words, nature and character of Christ.

First of all, Jesus *saw* that there was a harvest. Many Christians cannot see a harvest; they see only a barren field of dirt. They think the only thing that will be accomplished in this field is getting dirty. The fear of getting dirty in the field keeps most Christians from having sight beyond sight, and keeps them from ever seeing the harvest.

The church's fear of getting dirty in the world has kept us separated from them for many years. The fear of being associated with sin or with sinful people; getting a little dirt under our fingernails, has and will always keep us from seeing God's harvest.

The fear of being associated with sin or with sinful people; getting a little dirt under our fingernails, has and will always keep us from seeing God's harvest.

Secondly, Jesus not only saw a harvest, he saw the possibility of a *plentiful* harvest. In his mind there was no lack of harvest, only a lack of laborers. He thought the lack of laborers so great that he commanded his disciples to pray that God would *force out* and *thrust* laborers into the field.

You Can Lead A Horse To Water . . .

But even if laborers are forced out and thrust into the field, God cannot force them to have enough spiritual sight and vision to reap anything. We must begin to pray that God would not only send his laborers and place them in the field, but also that he would open their eyes – eyes that have long been blinded by religious spirits - and allow them to see the potential that lies in the field. Next, Jesus was moved with compassion for the people. If you truly desire to talk with a "vision-less" Christian, find one who is void of compassion. Sin-fearing, judgmental, condemning, homophobic Christians will never see the field or become laborers for the harvest. Compassion is not only a key to having this new sight, it is essential to becoming an effective Christian.

Finally, when Jesus speaks of this group of sinful and worldly people, he says that they *are his* harvest. Jesus gives ownership of these people to God the Father. God literally owns these people. They are his harvest. They belong to him, and he considers them his children. Until we can see past sin, and see the possibility of a plentiful harvest of souls, we will never achieve the level of insight that belonged to Jesus.

You Give Love A Bad Name

A good example of someone who did not possess this sight beyond sight is the biblical character Jonah. In Jonah we see a man who is completely void of any ability to see the potential of a sinful group of people becoming a bountiful harvest. The city of Ninevah was as "green" a pasture as you will ever find.

As a child this story was presented to me as if the reason Jonah refused to go to Ninevah was because

sight beyond sight

Sin-fearing, judgmental, condemning, homophobic Christians will never see the field or become laborers for the harvest.

he was afraid that the Ninevites were so wicked they would kill him. Upon further examination of the story we find that this was not Jonah's biggest reservation about going to Ninevah. His main problem with it was that he knew if he preached God's message of grace to them, God would indeed forgive these people who were so violent by nature. Despite his own failures, God chose Jonah to be his vessel to reach these hurting people. However, although Jonah, himself, had been a recipient of God's grace, he did not want to share it with others.

In my opinion, Jonah represents the majority of the church world today. He knew that God had commissioned him to go to a sinful group of people (the world), but his reluctance lay in his pharisaical fear that God would actually forgive them, forcing him to accept these people, who were so distasteful to him, as brothers and sisters in Christ. I see the spirit of Jonah alive and well when I watch many television preachers today who are so ready for the Lord to return. It is so obvious that in their zeal for this event to take place, their desire for him to judge a sinful world far outweighs their desire for him to affirm his love for his chosen people. This desire could not be further from the nature and character of God, whose wish is that none should perish.

These preachers continually try to justify themselves by likening the world today to Sodom and Gomorrah deeming it "unsavable." They wrongly assume they have done their part to show this world the merciful, compassionate, forgiving Christ, when in reality all they have offered the world is condemnation and judgmentalism.

When you read in Matthew 11:23, 24 what Jesus says about Sodom and Gomorrah it is clear who is *really* in danger of his judgment. He offers forgiveness and salvation to the unbelievers in Sodom and Gomorrah, but assures judgment for those who were knowledge-able of his works, holding them accountable for their actions. In other words, he forgives the sinners be-cause they didn't know any better. But he judges the church, because not only did they know better, they refused to help the unbelievers to "know better," which in God's eyes, is obviously a worse sin than anything the unbelievers were doing. *"For him who knows to do good and does it not, to him it is a sin."* The church should be very careful when we pray for judgment to come to those who deserve it. We may be bringing it down on our own heads!

The church should be very careful when we pray for judgment to come to those who deserve it. We may be bringing it down on our own heads.

Remember The Pit

The amazing thing about Jonah is that while inside the belly of the great fish he prays this prayer: *". . . Yet You have brought up my life from the pit, O Lord, my God* (Jonah 2:6)." When he's in trouble and in the midst of being corrected and chastised by God, he remembers how God has forgiven him of his transgressions. However, after God hears his prayer and delivers him; after he has been vomited onto the sand, he soon forgets his pit, and grows angry with God because the people of Ninevah have repented and have received forgiveness.

Isaiah instructs us how to be righteous when he says, *"Listen to me, you who follow after righteousness, you who seek the Lord: Look to the rock from which you were hewn, and to the hole of the pit from which you were dug" (Isaiah 51:1).* True righteousness does not come from our conduct or from our ability to follow a set of rules. The man or woman who desires to be righteous, must first look to his creator, God, *the rock from which they were hewn.*

Secondly, they must remember the pit that God has pulled them from and the sin for which he has forgiven them. We are told in the Word of God that he forgives our sins and remembers them no more. However, we are never instructed to forget our own sin or the pit from which God's grace has brought us. One of Jonah's downfalls was not remembering his pit.

It is important to note that Jonah was a Jew, and the Jewish people, at that time, were very nationalistic. As his chosen covenant people they felt they should have exclusive rights to God, and many had no intention of sharing him with the Gentiles. While Jonah's biggest fear should have been his disobedience to God's command to reach out to the Gentile city of Ninevah, it was not. Instead, he feared that a sinful and hasty people would be forgiven of their transgressions and be brought into the covenant that he and the other *chosen of God* did not want to share.

Asleep In The Light

Unlike Jesus, Jonah did not have *sight beyond sight*. He wasn't even close. In an attempt to run away from God's assignment to him to go to Ninevah, he got on a ship going to Tarshish. A great storm came and all the other men on the ship, who did not even know his God, were fighting for their lives. But Jonah was asleep. They had to cry out to him to wake him up in the midst of the storm to help them try to save the ship.

I can't help but feel that sometimes while the world cries out for help in the midst of the storm, the church, like Jonah, sleeps. It's difficult to sleep with a light shining in your eyes, but somehow the church manages to do it. We know the truth. We have the *Light*. We know to do good. We know that our assignment, our commission, is to reach out to the sinner, yet we continue to sleep in the bottom of the ship, while all the lost, hurting people are crying out to us to help them through the storm. We sleep when we put God

...while the world cries out for help in the midst of the storm, the church, like Jonah, sleeps.

61

*There is no
lack of har-
vest. There is
no lack of
laborers.
There is only a
lack of labor-
ers who have
sight to see
the harvest!*

into a box, and don't believe that he can love us and another group of people, who may be very different from us, at the same time. It may come as a startling realization to some in the church, but God is big enough to go around! Even though millions upon millions may respond to his grace, each of us can have as much interaction with him in our personal lives as we want. While we as humans think in finite terms, he is infinite, and so is his ability to love and accept us – *all* of us.

There is no lack of harvest today. There is no lack of laborers. There is only a lack of laborers who have sight to see the harvest! Please don't sleep through the storm. Wake up and listen to the cries of those around you. Ask God to give you *sight beyond sight* to see them not as miserable sinners, but as potential followers of Christ.

NO TRESPASSING

As a child, I grew up in a subdivision of houses surrounding a 5-acre lake. When I was old enough, I began to fish in this lake and developed a love for the outdoors and for fishing. One day a close friend of mine asked me if I wanted to go fishing. I immediately said, "sure," and we were off.

When the car came to a stop, my friend got out and began to get his gear out of the trunk. I opened the door and said, "Where is the lake?" He replied, "Oh, it's just a short walk through those woods." I realized later that *short* was a relative term. I reluctantly got out of the car and gathered my gear for the walk to the lake. After walking for about half a mile I began noticing some *No Trespassing* signs. In fact, I had never seen so many notices declaring a landowner's desire for privacy.

After trekking through the woods a while longer we finally came upon the lake, and my friend turned to me and whispered, "O.K., we can fish now, but when you cast, try to stand behind the closest tree so you won't be spotted."

Now, my daddy didn't raise no fool! I was not stupid enough to think that this was the latest and most innovative, revolutionary technique of " hiding from the fish." I thought this a little suspicious, so I asked, "Why?" My friend answered, "Because the old man who owns this property will come out of his house shooting if he sees anyone fishing in his lake. Well "all-righty" then! Thanks for telling me in time to change my mind about coming!

Now, I realized that *stupid* is also a relative term. I did value my young life, but it was too late. I had already tasted the excitement of a fish grabbing my lure, and this was a new lake with new fish that were not accustomed to my lure. My heart raced! Standing behind the nearest tree I cast my trusty rooster tail lure into the forbidden water. Bingo! Within two or three cranks I landed the biggest Largemouth Bass I have ever caught to this day.

'Gimme Three Steps

In my excitement I screamed to my friend, "Hey! Look what I caught!" Instead of replying, he glared at me with a look that instantly conveyed the message, "You idiot, why are you screaming? Don't you remember that we are trespassing on a crazy, trigger happy old man's land?" The next sound I heard was that of a door slamming in the distance. I expected the next sound to be that of gunfire. Instead I saw five or six angry looking dogs running down the hill toward us at full speed. Even worse!!! We immediately dropped our fishing poles, my freshly caught trophy still attached, and ran for our lives. I still don't know how those dogs did not catch us, but I wasn't going back to find out.

I decided after this experience that I would return to the lake in my backyard. Needless to say, it was the safe and sane choice. But I soon grew tired of catching only small fish, and weary of trying to trick the larger ones to bite. You see, the lake where I lived was open to the whole community, and the older, bigger fish had grown smarter and smarter with every fisherman and every lure. Occasionally, I would catch a fish big enough to be considered a "keeper," but almost without exception I would notice a number of holes and scars surrounding the perimeter of the mouths of these fish. This was not the first time these fish had been caught. It dawned on me then why the old man who owned that lake with the big fish had so many *No Trespassing* signs posted. It was because he had his lake stocked and did not want any trespassers coming in taking his big fish out. If I had never left the lake behind my house, I would not know that there were other lakes to fish in, and other fish to be caught – perhaps even bigger fish!

If I had never left the lake behind my house, I would not know that there were other lakes to fish in, and other fish to be caught - perhaps even bigger fish!

65

*...just because
we are to be
fishers of men
does not mean
that we all
must fish in
the same
pond!*

Deep Blue Sea

We see in the Bible that Jesus took common, ordinary fishermen and made them into *fishers of men*. Any self-respecting Christian would admit that part of our duty, as children of God, is to become a fisher of men. It sounds simple doesn't it? But it's often easier said than done. Innate within most born again Christians is the desire to see others come to the knowledge of Christ and to experience the new birth. However, just because we are to be fishers of men does not mean that we all must fish in the same pond!

I have had the chance to go deep-sea fishing twice in my life. The first time I went, I was with the father of a girlfriend of mine. Everything was first class. There were only four others on the boat and each person had plenty of space to cast and to operate. He was paying! My second experience was not so pleasant largely due to the fact that I was paying for it myself and tried the cheaper alternative of paying $20 for a 50-person charter. There were too many people on the boat, with too little space. When someone happened to catch a fish, nine times out of ten his line became tangled with the person's next to him.

The problem we faced on that trip was not that there were not enough fish in the ocean. The problem was not that the ocean was too small for all of us to fish in. The problem was that we all decided to fish in the same spot. The church of today faces the same problem. It is not that there are not plenty of unsaved people out there. It is not that there is no new territory to be gained for the Kingdom of God. It is that the church is so narrow-minded in its approach that we wait for them to come to us. We will not pay the price to acquire the expensive boat so that we can launch out into the deep to catch the really big ones. Instead, we all crowd around each other on the cheap, convenient 50-person charter, saturating one little spot with so many lures that the fish just look up and laugh at us spending all our time untangling our lines and fighting over miniscule amounts of what we consider prime ministry space.

When I see churches competing with each other to see who can get the most members it sickens me because I know that most of the *new* members being added to one church's role have not yet had their names deleted from the books at their last church. We are not adding new members. We are simply accepting "church hoppers" who run around from church to church trying to get their blessing. It is amazing to me that between 75-80% of people who join Charismatic churches are not new converts. They are merely disgruntled, immature people transferring their membership from one place to another every six months or so.

...75-80% of people who join Charismatic Churches are not new converts. They are merely disgruntled, immature people transferring their membership from one place to another...

67

These people will never be a stable force in any church. They will never be pillars in a church because they have no foundation. Because they refuse to put down any type of respectable root system they become "spiritual tumbleweeds" being blown around by every wind of doctrine and being attracted by every new fad that comes into the church.

These people are like the fish that I caught in my lake growing up. They all have an impressive array of holes in their mouths. They have been caught before by some other fisherman; or should I say some other fast talking, prosperity-promising preacher. And this will probably not be the last time they are caught! Whenever the next lure comes along, they will surely bite again.

This cycle will continue as long as churches right down the street from each other refuse to try anything new, and all keep fishing in the same little pond. They may get fancy every now and then and use a new and different lure, but rest assured, the fish will grow wise to all of them sooner or later.

Livin' La Vida Loca

Preaching that is popular today includes crazy lures of all kinds. There is the "prosperity" lure that tricks the fish into biting because it promises instantaneous debt reduction, but only after listening to the tape series which costs $49.95. There is the "Jesus could return tonight" lure that attracts those who are tired of living in this God-forsaken, sinful world. To get in on this one, all you have to do is buy a kit ensuring your *rapture readiness*. There is the "stand up and be a responsible man" lure that attempts to take us back to the law through spiritual pride. Never mind that this one comes dangerously close to *trampling under foot the blood of Christ*, and causing his death to be in vain. There is also the trusty "fear and condemnation" lure that scares the fish into biting or else!

Attempts to have the biggest church on the street have caused almost every preacher to throw out one or more of these lures. When the bigger, more influential fish become wise to these tactics, they head for deeper water, which leaves the church fighting over the small, young, dumb fish who offer little more than large amounts of irrelevant and misguided zeal.

The central message of the gospels is this: accept the free gift of forgiveness offered through Christ's

Attempts to have the biggest church on the street have caused almost every preacher to throw out one or more of these lures.

69

finished work of grace. Christ's finished work on the cross implies that we can do without preachers who act as task-masters, trying to force people to work for their "undeserved" forgiveness. The only thing this does is push people back into the law, and deeper into the clutches of sin and death!

I believe the time has come for the church to cast our nets on the other side. It is time that we practice some common sense, and find some new ponds. Only then will we snag the ones who have never been caught before. The only lure that is sure to work in any pond and on any fish is a gospel that really is *good news.*

I Double Dog Dare You

On our voyage to the deeper water of new ponds - the greener pastures of new territory - we will encounter many *No Trespassing* signs. By this I mean that on this voyage certain types of people, types of people that the church has traditionally steered clear of, might cross our path. When we begin to encounter them our instinct tells us that we are on strange and unfamiliar ground where we should not *trespass.* We might come across a homosexual in this pond. In this pond may be an adulterer. This pond may be home to a young lady who has had an abortion. Or, God forbid, this pond could possibly contain a person who does not know anything about Jesus, or someone who believes in a different god. Keep out! *No Trespassing!* Jesus Christ did not simply pass by these *No Trespassing* zones; he took up residence in these forbidden places! He spent his life and ministry trespassing into places where the religious order would dare not enter.

If we can put aside our reputations and fear of the unknown enough to travel to some new ponds and cast our nets on the other side, the catch would be so tremendous that our nets would begin to break, forcing us to call on other *fishermen* of like vision to help with the overflow. And the fish we would catch then would not have mouths full of holes from previous catches. They would truly be new converts for the Kingdom of God!

Just The Facts Ma'am

An important thing to realize at this point is that in order to fish in the deep water we must put down our fishing rods, for they are created to catch only one fish at a time. We must adapt our fishing style to use a net, which is the only method capable of catching a large amount of fish. Matthew 13:47 speaks of the Kingdom of God being like a *dragnet* that is thrown out for the purpose of collecting *some of every kind*. We have never been smart enough, or courageous enough to fish in the kind of water that requires a dragnet. But that is where the incredibly large fish

Jesus Christ did not simply pass by these no trespassing zones; He took up residence in these forbidden places.

swim; the ones who can bring immediate influence and financial resources to the Kingdom of God. I say we gather up our gear, trespass on some land and fish from the all the ponds that Satan has scared us away from for so many years. The reality of the Kingdom of God can never be fulfilled as long as all the trophy-sized fish are still hanging over Satan's mantle. It's time to get them back.

**finding sacred
in the secular**

SHEEP IN WOLVES' CLOTHING

"In the beginning, throughout the universe, there was a deep and abiding sense of peace. There was great joy and liberty. Everything was in its right place, and every creature worshipped the Lord. One among us, the most lovely among us, was called Lucifer, and in him God found great pleasure. For it was given to Lucifer the gift of beautiful worship. And how he did worship with his instruments and with the dance, and how God loved him.

"But Lucifer became exalted because of his talent, and he desired to be worshipped even as God is worshipped. So he gathered his forces together, purposing in his heart to establish his own kingdom equal to God's. And the Lord knew it and said, 'Lucifer, because you have craved my high places which do not belong to you, you are banished to the depths," and God cast him and his followers to earth."

This is the opening narration of a play we wrote and presented at our church several years ago entitled *Restoring That Which Was Lost.* The play tells the biblical story found in both Isaiah 14 and in Revelation 12 where Lucifer, who was originally created as an angel of worship, rebelled against God and caused a war in heaven between the angels. He was then

*The underlying
theme in all of
recorded history
as we know it has
been about this
struggle for
power and
dominion over
the earth, and as
Christians, we are
left with the
incredible
responsibility of
responding to
one fundamental
question: "Who's
in charge?"*

*Satan is alive and
well in world sys-
tems, and the
church poses no
viable threat to
him or to the posi-
tion he holds there
as long as we re-
main inside our
four walls, void of
anything resem-
bling influence in
world systems.*

cast down to the earth along with all the angels who had sided with him against God and his name became Satan. Ever since his rebellion and fall, a struggle for authority and power has existed in God's universe. He no longer has a position in heaven. His position, power, rule and authority have been confined to earth by God, himself.

The underlying theme in all of recorded history as we know it has been about this struggle for power and dominion over the earth, and as Christians, we are left with the incredible responsibility of responding to one fundamental question: "Who's in charge?" Jesus is literally held in the heavens until his church can successfully return all power and authority to God *("'til his enemies are made his footstool" Matthew 22:44 / I Corinthians 15:24-25 / Hebrews 10:12-13).*

Any authority Satan has in the earth must be facilitated through world systems. World systems do not recognize the importance of relying on God. World systems are a "law unto themselves," recognizing no authority greater than their own. Any system that does not recognize God as creator of this universe is an authority that must be dealt with. Satan is alive and well in world systems, and the church poses no viable threat to him or to the position he holds there as long as the we remain inside our four walls, void of anything resembling influence in world systems.

In his wisdom, God has decided to limit himself at times to working only through us. This strategy can be problematic because it is dependent upon the same principle that created the possibility for Satan's rebellion and for original sin - free will!

The success of this strategy rests in our ability to realize that through Christ in us, the hope of glory, we must make the choice to *willingly* enter into these systems of the world, or "anti-authorities," to God, and regain in his name the authority that belongs to and originated from him. It is our job to *restore* that which was lost on the earth.

So how do we make his enemies his footstool? Our *task* is to successfully get behind enemy lines and regain the influence and authority Satan has stolen from the Kingdom of God. Our *strategy* is to have highly effective camouflage so that we may enter this territory *undetected.* As Christ sends us out as *sheep among wolves,* we must realize that we are going into enemy territory. Blending in with our surrounding environment is crucial to our mission and to our survival. We must appear to be as wolves among wolves, all the while retaining our identity and character as sheep and followers of Christ. We must become *sheep in wolves' clothing.*

Our strategy is to have highly effective camouflage so that we may enter this territory undetected.

finding sacred
in the secular

chapter seven

SHEEP IN WOLVES' CLOTHING

The Bible uses the analogy of sheep to describe followers of Christ. As sheep we should be watchful and constantly on the lookout for wolves disguised in sheep's clothing. This statement has been repeated and preached by thousands of preachers from many different pulpits to many different congregations. This concept is certainly not evil; it is simply defensive in nature.

Who's Afraid of the Big Bad Wolf?

And he huffed, and he puffed, and he blew their house down! Like the three little pigs, many Christians spend their time wondering how they can avoid being gobbled up by Satan, *the Big Bad Wolf*. Misreading scripture about watching out for wolves in sheep's clothing has instigated fear in the hearts of believers for many years.

Fear has a way of making you freeze. How many of us have experienced this kind of fear late at night, alone in the house, when we think we have heard footsteps downstairs? All of the sudden we become too afraid to do anything. And although we have rehearsed in our minds hundreds of times grabbing our gun or baseball bat, we now seem to be paralyzed by

*We have been
paralyzed by
fear, and have
remained in
the church
pulling the
cover up over
our heads,
attempting to
hide our-
selves.*

fear and the only defense that comes to mind is one that instinctively arises from our childhood - pulling the cover up over our head and hiding. After all, everybody knows bullets can't penetrate bed sheets!

This has been the reaction of Christians for years to the possibility that *Big Bad Wolf* Satan will come in among us and steal our sheep. We too have been paralyzed by fear, and have remained in the church pulling the cover up over our heads, attempting to hide ourselves.

Hide and Seek

The present *hiding mode* of the church has created somewhat of a *catch 22*. First of all, it does not allow us to be found by the people who need our help. Neither does it allow us to see what is going on around us. When we are in this fearful mode of hiding, it is impossible for us to be aware of the society that surrounds us, and thus we are unable to reach the lost who are held captive in this world's systems. They can't see us, and we can't see them. Great plan!

The phrase "the best defense is a good offense" has probably been uttered by every coach since the existence of sports of any kind. But there's a reason for that – it's true. We have allowed Satan to frighten us to the point where we cower inside the four walls of the church, constantly remaining on the defense. For the benefit of the athletically challenged let me insert at this point that you cannot score when you are on the defense. If you find yourself behind and on the defense when the final seconds of the game clock are ticking down, there is no possible way for you to win. The best that you can hope for is a tie. And everybody knows how horribly anticlimactic ties are.

As long as we remain in a defensive mode, we will never achieve victory. The Bible tells us that *the Kingdom suffers violence, and the violent take it by force.* I do not believe that we will ever be perceived as a violent-spirited people, eagerly seeking to establish God's Kingdom by allowing fear to paralyze us and keep us hiding in the church with the cover of religion and tradition pulled up over our heads.

Although many Christians do not agree with this, Satan is extremely smart, attractive and strategic! The Bible describes him as the most *beautiful* and *cunning* creature of the field. He will not be defeated simply by our *stomping* on him symbolically during a church service. His defeat does not lie in our ability to *rebuke* him. He will not be scared away by us waving our handkerchiefs or by our wearing brightly colored suits. Victory over Satan will be ours only when we go into his territory and reclaim all that he has stolen from the Kingdom of God.

...Satan is extremely smart, attractive and strategic! ...He will not be defeated simply by our stomping on him symbolically during a church service.

81

Keep Your Eye on the Ball

If Satan cannot *destroy* us he will seek to *distract* us. Allowing ourselves to be distracted by fear can be every bit as bad as being destroyed. In either case, our paralytic condition has frozen us into a state of *suspended animation*. Our ministry to the world has come to a complete stop. Fear can be an incredible distraction that acts as a destructive device on the body of Christ.

We cannot continue to believe that the answer to ending Satan's reign of terror in world systems is as easy as someone walking into a corporate building rebuking all of the evil spirits present there, causing them to flee. We will never defeat him by standing on the steps of our state capitols declaring "all out war" against his powers and principalities; especially if we leave there only to return to our religious games of playing church and receiving our blessing. And we cannot continue to believe that by assembling our youth groups and smashing all of our secular CD's we are destroying his hold on the world of entertainment.

In order to score, the offense must enter the defense's territory.

As long as we rely on methods such as these we are still playing defense! We must vow to discontinue our fear-driven, defensive strategies and become *offensive* minded. In order to score, the offense must enter the defense's territory. So how do we go into Satan's domain and reclaim all that we have lost? By being smarter than him! We must go into world systems as *sheep in wolves' clothing*. This strategy is the exact opposite of hiding in the church, looking out for the would-be wolves coming in to devour the flock.

When in Rome

I feel that I need to interject here that having a violent spirit does not mean gathering up arms and assembling a small militia with plans to take over the world. We are not called to be followers of David Koresh. We are, however, instructed in Matthew 10:16 to go out as *sheep among the wolves*. In this same verse we hear Christ again talking about how plentiful the harvest is. Again we hear him pleading with God to send out laborers into *his* harvest. God answers by devising the strategy of *the seventy*. This strategy is to send out seventy of Jesus' disciples, two by two into every city to which he would travel. He gives these seventy very specific instructions as to how to conduct themselves while in these cities.

Yes, he sends them out as lambs among wolves, but he does not instruct them to *act* as lambs. In fact, the strategy he gives them is closer to that of a wise serpent. He does not insist on them letting the people in the house in which they are staying know they are his disciples, but on the contrary, instructs them to act as the people in that particular city would act.

The next thing he tells them is to eat and drink whatever is set before them and to follow the customs of that house. It is interesting to note that he tells them to stay in the houses of the everyday people who live in these cities. He does not tell them to preach repentance on the street corners or, even better, to pass out *turn or burn* evangelistic tracts. He simply wants them to establish relationships. He instructs them to blend in with their surroundings, which is the hallmark of the principle I call *sheep in wolves' clothing*.

She's A Brick House

In the story of Esther we see a perfect example of someone becoming a *sheep in wolves' clothing*. To me, Esther is one of the most unique women in the Bible. Because many people read her story with religious eyes, they miss the powerful truth it reveals.

Esther, who was an adopted orphan, seems to be a very unlikely candidate to be the savior of her entire nation. It was not her family heritage or her spiritual insight that brought her into the king's chamber. It was her beauty and fleshly appeal. Once Esther had been chosen as one of the virgins who was to be brought before King Ahasuerus, she immediately set herself apart from the rest of the pack. She did this by identifying the king's weaknesses and capitalizing on them.

The King's first noticeable weakness was his desire for submission. He had wanted his former Queen, Vashti, to come and show herself and her beauty to his constituents, but she refused. This act of rebellion so infuriated him that he made a public decree that Vashti would no longer be allowed to come before him, and her crown would be given to another. And it was understood that the new queen would have to be someone who was comfortable wholly submitting herself to him as king. Even his insistence on interviewing only virgins for the position of the new queen was a subtle clue to his desire for submission. He wanted them untouched and uninhibited by the control of any other man. This clue did not go unnoticed by Esther.

The King's second obvious weakness was for beautiful women. After the King had assembled this group of young, beautiful virgins, he was very specific about the "beauty preparations" that were to be given to them before they could have an audience (or rendezvous) with him. Each woman was to bathe for six months in oil of myrrh. Another six months was devoted to perfumes and "preparations for beautifying women." One entire year of bathing and perfuming! I think it's safe to say that this king was concerned about the smell of his women. Apparently, King Ahasuerus had a prior experience with a woman whose personal hygiene was inadequate.

Because she had identified these weaknesses of the King's, Esther set out to become the most submissive and desirous woman in the group. She succeeded. To show her submission, Esther requested nothing but what the King's eunuch suggested to her. After bathing and perfuming herself for a year for this man, she could have given his eunuch a little attitude. She could have used her incredible beauty to take advantage of the situation. But she was smart enough to realize that the King would be more impressed with her submissive attitude and her *low maintenance* approach, than with demands.

After her response to the eunuch, the Bible records that she gained *favor with all who saw her* in the King's palace. She was not only concerned with the King's perception of her; she wanted to gain influence with all those who surrounded him.

Esther's ability to find favor with him was completely dependent upon her ability to conceal her identity...

The Missionary's Position
Esther would now face the biggest challenge of her mission - finding favor in the sight of King Ahasuerus. Her ability to find favor with him was completely dependent upon her ability to conceal her identity as a

Jew and upon her ability to please King Ahasuerus
by any means necessary.

Esther again was successful. She did find favor in
the King's sight and he esteemed her more highly
than all of the other women. So much so that the
King named Esther queen in Vashti's place, placed
the royal crown on her head, called a feast in her
honor and set aside a day that would be considered
a holiday in her name.

Allow me to be carnal-minded for a moment. No man
in his right mind goes to the extent that this King did
to give honor to a woman in return for *good conver-
sation.* Call me crazy, but I think Esther did more than
talk about politics in the King's chamber. She did
something that drove this man wild. And I doubt that
as she worked her magic on him she remained in the
missionary position. No way! She was fighting for
the lives of her people, the whole Jewish nation, and
this may have been her only shot. Believe me, she
did everything she could think of. But she also allowed her disguise to remain in tact until she had
gained the necessary influence and favor in the King's
sight. Maybe I can say it more clearly — Esther did
not reveal her true identity as a Hebrew girl until she
had King Ahasuerus thoroughly "whipped" in the bedroom! Enough said?

*...she also
allowed her
disguise to
remain in tact
until she had
gained the
necessary
influence and
favor in the
King's sight.*

Although she did not reveal her identity to anyone in the King's palace, she continued secret communication with her people. The success of her mission depended a great deal on her communication and relationship with Mordecai, her adoptive father who is representative of a spiritual father and advisor in the story. Mordecai had instructed Esther not to reveal her identity until she was in the proper *position* to do so.

We Will Serve No Wine Before Its Time

For a younger generation to successfully enter the systems of this world and gain influence without being destroyed or swallowed up, it will take some spiritual Mordecai's to advise them on strategy and timing. However, Mordecai almost destroyed all of Esther's careful work when he dressed himself in sackcloth and paraded himself around the King's court announcing his concern for Esther. Mordecai's refusal to bow to Haman almost blew the cover of Esther's mission as well. The spiritual Mordecai's of the future must be very sensitive and careful not to expose *Esther's* identity in world systems too soon.

*The spiritual
Mordecai's of
the future
must be very
sensitive and
careful not to
expose
Esther's
identity in
world systems
too soon.*

Esther's ability to know the proper time to reveal her identity is a mark of spiritual maturity not readily found in the church today. We must learn from Esther's example how to blend in with our surroundings and gain influence. Just as surely as the salvation of the Jewish nation depended upon Esther's ability to conceal her identity, the restoration of God's world depends on our ability to be as sheep in wolves' clothing, concealing our identity until the proper time.

Many people don't realize it, but the name of God is not mentioned one time throughout the entire book of Esther. The hand of God is so evident, however, that most people never notice. This is a good example of letting your actions speak louder than your words, or your attempts at witnessing. The story of Esther's life is the best example I can offer of how the body of Christ must handle themselves when interacting in world systems.

If we, the body of Christ, remain paralyzed by the fear of *wolves in sheep's clothing*, we will never leave the bondage of defensive thinking. We must become offensive minded and go into the world as *sheep in wolves' clothing*. We must learn to fit in, find the weaknesses and act appropriately to take advantage of the favor that will be offered to us.

finding sacred
in the secular

chapter eight

SURVIVAL OF THE FITTEST

Survival of the fittest is a non-technical term for the process of natural selection, which is one of the components of Charles Darwin's theory of evolution. Although I am a Christian and believe God is the divine creator and originator of the universe, I still recognize that there are truths to be gleaned from other ways of thinking. Many people, however, will not engage their minds in something that is foreign to them because they fear being converted to some other belief system. Our strongest sense of security lies in what we believe.

Relax! I do not believe that we crawled out of a plasma pool and eventually gained conscious thought. As I have stated, I believe that God is the divine creator and architect of the universe. But I have often wondered why so many Christians are adamantly opposed to engaging in discussion with people of other beliefs. After all, we have the truth don't we? Then why are we so scared? When people are fearful of having an open mind it is usually because deep inside they know they cannot give an adequate defense for what they believe.

Any good debate teacher will force his or her students to argue both sides of an issue. They do this because they know that being familiar with both extremes provides perspective, and will assist in preparing a defense of their own position.

Perspective is key when attempting to find common ground with someone who does not share your beliefs. The mistake most Christians make in this situation is thinking that arguing long enough and loud enough will eventually result in winning someone to the Lord. People are not won to Christ through argument or debate. But we can engage them by finding common ground with them, something we can agree on. This is the strength of having perspective: finding common ground.

*People are not
won to Christ
through
argument or
debate. But
we can engage
them by
finding com-
mon ground...*

No religion other than Christianity offers grace as an answer to sin. They may offer a way for you to "do it yourself," but they do not offer a free gift of salvation through belief in a *finished work*. Despite this, there are many truths with which we can find common ground in other religions. For example, along with the Buddhists we can affirm the value of all forms of life and respect for God's creation. True Buddhists are not to blame for the environmental problems in the world, we Christians are. Likewise, from the theory of evolution we can learn how *survival of the fittest* or natural selection can offer a fresh perspective and a practical strategy for the adaptation and survival of the church in this next millennium.

Does Not Nature Teach You?

The word of God asks us, "Does not nature teach you?" When we look at the process of natural selection, we find some very interesting things. The very definition of natural selection speaks multitudes to those who have *ears to hear.* Webster's definition of natural selection is *"in evolution, the process by which those individuals (of a species) with characters that help them to become **adapted to their specific environment tend to leave more progeny and transmit their characters, while those less able to become adapted tend to leave fewer progeny or die out,** so that in the course of generations there is a progressive tendency in the species to a greater degree of adaptation."*

When we begin to dissect this definition we see terms like: *adaptation, progeny, generations* and *die out.*

Adaptation involves blending in with your surroundings; adapting, if you will—camouflaging— which is necessary to surviving in any environment. Adaptation is a vital skill in the process of becoming *sheep in wolves clothing.* For the church to survive we must learn to change or adapt as our environment and society changes. We must find new ways and strategies to reach the lost. The speed at which we are

The speed at which we are able to adapt will not only determine our survival, but also the survival of the generations to follow.

able to adapt will not only determine our survival, but also the survival of the generations to follow.

Progeny is simply a word used for offspring, descendants, lineage or family. If we can learn to adapt so that we are relevant to our society then our progeny will be much greater. This generation's ability to adapt and be relevant in our world and its ever-changing needs will determine the ability of our offspring to have influence. In religious terms, if we learn to adapt to our world's needs we can "save" more people and enlarge the number of citizens in the Kingdom of God.

Generations is obviously a term suggesting something that continues beyond itself. We see in the Bible that there are blessings and curses that may be *generational*. If we don't adapt to the needs of our society, our descendants, the generations who will follow us, will be cursed, having nothing to inherit; and the church that has survived for two thousand years could very well *die out.*

We must begin to take a closer look at our ability to adapt to the world we live in. We must become the voice of solution in an environment of chaos. The Bible speaks of people having the ability to predict or forecast the weather, yet having no knowledge of the *season* that they live in. Trends, moods and seasons in society change rapidly. Sadly, the church usually does not recognize the change or make any effort to

*Sadly, the
church usually
does not
recognize the
change or
make any
effort to adapt
until the trend
has already
changed
again.*

adapt until the trend has already changed again. As long as we continue this pattern, our progeny will be scarce.

Predator or Prey?

As we study nature, we see that every living thing survives from the existence of other living things. Every species fits into what we call the *food chain*. Some animals live at the top of the food chain and have few or no predators. Others live at the bottom of the food chain and must consider every other animal a possible predator. Their very existence depends on their defense mechanisms. The animals at the bottom of the food chain never seem to have a moment's peace. They are constantly in defensive or survival mode, while the animals living at the top of the food chain simply stroll or swim around, being viewed respectfully by every other creature.

Where does the body of Christ presently fit in the food chain of society? Are we destined merely to *survive* at the bottom? Will we forever be the animal who must survive by our defensive thinking? Or will we adapt quickly enough to be greatly respected by the society in which we exist?

For too long the church has managed to *scrape by* in survival mode. The Kingdom of God will not be es-

Where does the body of Christ presently fit in the food chain of society? ...will we adapt quickly enough to be greatly respected by the society in which we exist?

95

tablished by a defensive or survivalist mentality. We must begin to think *revival* instead of *survival*. When the body of Christ is mature enough to discern the times and seasons of society before they pass, we will sit at the top of the food chain, gaining respect from all those who see us.

All Things To All People

True revival is not merely marked by long, consecutive church services. Revival is marked by the masses of people who give their lives to Christ. The number of that mass is completely dependent on our ability to adapt our approach to be relevant to them. The skill of adaptation is a necessity for the church to be relevant in modern society.

The number of that mass (of people who give their lives to Christ) is completely dependent on our ability to adapt our approach to be relevant to them.

Adaptation should not to be confused with compromise. In I Corinthians 9:19-23, the Apostle Paul models for us the way to adapt to any environment we may find ourselves in. He suggests that we learn to *become all things to all people* so that by any means we may share the gospel. While doing this, however, he also mentions that he is never without law toward God in his heart. By making the gospel relevant to society we are not compromising it, we are enhancing it. We are making it come alive. We are ensuring more progeny!

In Psalm 102:18-20, David prophesies of a generation to come, a people who are *"yet to be created"* who will hear the groaning of the earth. I believe that generation is here. As we become sensitive to our society and to the *season* in which we live, David's prophecy is fulfilled.

finding sacred
in the secular

chapter nine

SEPARATE BUT EQUAL

Separate but equal is a phrase that was created during the Civil Rights movement by those who did not want public schools to become racially integrated. The argument offered by white segregationists was that the public schools attended by black children were equipped with the same facilities and materials as the public schools attended by white children. So why not keep them separate? Why rock the boat by integrating?

Play That Funky Music White Boy

As a member of the Concerned Clergy and of the Atlanta Christian Council, my uncle, Archbishop Earl P. Paulk, Jr. was assigned to investigate the matter. He surveyed several of the schools attended by white children and found their classrooms, books, gymnasiums, laboratories and overall facilities in excellent condition, equipped with everything necessary to ensure quality education.

He also took a survey of several different schools attended by black children and what he found was extremely shocking. In most cases, all of the students, ranging from 5 to 18 years of age, were usually crowded into one classroom. Often, no running water was available to the children, and if there was a bathroom at all, it was outdoors. Their textbooks consisted of hand-me-downs from the white schools and were usually torn, out of date and irrelevant. In all cases, there were no central heating devices, meaning that in cold weather the children were forced to huddle around a fire or pot-bellied stove to keep warm.

He reported back to the group what he had found and voiced his obvious concerns, that the black schools and the white schools in the state were certainly *separate*, but definitely not *equal*. When word of this *concern* reached the governor of Georgia he reportedly vowed, "I'll close the schools before I'll allow them to be integrated."

The Concerned Clergy and the Atlanta Christian Council then wrote a manifesto stating the vast difference between the conditions of the schools and thus their decision to advocate integration. My uncle and my father, Pastor Don L. Paulk, helped to write and signed this manifesto. As a result of this and the efforts of other groups, public schools in Georgia began the slow process of integration within the next several years.

That was Then, This is Now

This phrase, *separate but equal*, typifies the relation-ship between the world and the church today. Equally, all people are God's children, but separated from each other by religious tradition and fear. There are segre-gationists at work in the church today who would rather close the church than see it open its doors to a sinful and hurting humanity!

Dr. Martin Luther King, Jr. once said, "Sunday morn-ing is the most segregated hour of the week." Throughout the years since his death, this statement has slowly become less and less true as many pas-tors have attempted to create and maintain interra-cial congregations. The church I was raised in and now pastor in, The Cathedral of the Holy Spirit, was a pioneer of this vision and a demonstration of the real-ity of black people and white people attending the same church beginning in the 1960's.

But that was forty years ago! We must now take a step beyond racial integration in our churches. We are called upon today to swing the doors of the church wide open to all people of the world. The most segre-gated hour of the week will remain on Sunday morn-ing as long as all of the *saved* are in church and all of the *sinners* are not welcome. You may say, "We can't force people to come to church." Well said. I agree with you. But if they won't come to church, let's take church to them.

When we talk about *taking church to the world* we must discard our paradigm of thinking this begins and ends with having "street meetings." These meetings are traditionally designed to reach out to drunks, homeless people, beggars, etc. Yes, it is our responsibility to care for these people but it is not the way to gain influence in world systems. Bars, streets, clubs are not world systems, they are places. For the most part our "street meetings" do more harm than good, because they serve only to give credence to the stereotype we have acquired of being pushy and paternalistic.

We Are Spirits in the Material World

Taking church to the "sinner" today must be married to a well devised strategy for gaining influence in the systems that entrap these people, not just shouting "Jesus loves you" from a street corner. Street meeting evangelism is not quite my idea of being *undetected*.

The reason many people will not come to church is because generations of church leaders have held to the idea that people must clean themselves up before they can come to church. That makes about as much sense as if you were to cut yourself, stop the flow of blood until a scab has formed, and *then* rush yourself to the emergency room. One of my uncle's favorite statements is, "The church is a hospital for sinners, not a country club for saints." Sometimes the church is even an emergency room. You don't overcome your sickness and then go to the doctor. You go to the doctor *because* you are sick! In order for us to destroy the stereotypes created by too many misinformed preachers, we must go into the world and establish relationships based on love and acceptance, rather than change or fear.

I know what most religious minds are thinking right now: "What about II Corinthians 6:17?" *Come out from among them and be separate?* If you take the time to read this entire chapter you will see that the Corinthians had allowed the worship of idols to infest their church. The church in Corinth made the grave error of allowing the *world* to influence them, rather than *them* influencing the world. We are to be *in* the world, not *of* the world; sheep in wolves' clothing, not wolves. As we are attempting to relate with those who have fallen into a pit we must remember at all times that we cannot pull them out of the pit if we fall in ourselves.

The task that lies in front of us is not for the weak minded or for those who are easily influenced. Peer pressure cannot be a factor to those who will be successful in this struggle. As I have stated before, children are not taken to battle. And neither should baby Christians be expected to fight in or survive it.

So Close, Yet So Far

To perform this mission of gaining influence in worldly places we must be as Daniel and the three Hebrew children, Shadrach, Meshach and Abed-Nego. They were considered good looking and intelligent young men. So much so, that after three years of training in the king's palace, they were appointed as his advisors. They had gained influence by learning the *in's and out's* of the system they were in, yet were not influenced by their surroundings, refusing to eat the food and drink the wine accessible to those in the palace.

They blended in with their surroundings even to the extent of allowing their names, their very identity to be changed. However, they succeeded in gaining the appropriate influence without serving another god or becoming enslaved by temptation.

Daniel and the others *learned* everything that this particular system of government had to offer, but they did not *believe* everything they learned! To successfully gain the type of influence that these young men had we must train and prepare our minds, and the minds of a younger generation, to learn everything possible about world systems. However, we must always remember that we are on a mission for God. We do not necessarily believe everything that we learn.

Worlds Apart

The term *separate but equal* no longer describes the schools in the South, but it perfectly describes the current segregationist relationship between the church and the world. We are all equally God's creation and his children, but we live in very separate worlds. Think for a moment how news of the sudden death of a family member, or a personal terminal condition effects believers and non-believers. A Christian who has a strong support system within his family and church would receive such news much differently than someone who does not know the love and grace of God. How selfish are we when we refuse to share that sense of peace and comfort with everyone we know?

I have had feelings of outrage, disbelief and anger, when I have seen and read depictions of the black schools prior to the Civil Rights Movement. I believe that every child should have the right to a quality education and to quality facilities. How much more should we be incensed at the current condition of the people in the world for whom Christ died? Is there not a cause? Is there no balm in Gilead? Can we not see that these hurting people are huddled together, around the "pot-bellied" stove, as it were, searching for the warmth of love and acceptance?

For the most part, the only knowledge of Christ that they have been offered is reminiscent of those 1960's hand-me-down textbooks from the white kids to the black kids. It is torn, outdated and irrelevant, and comes nowhere near properly representing the nature or person of Jesus Christ.

We Shall Overcome

It is time for people of like mind, spirit and vision to come together and create a new *manifesto,* a document to make the body of Christ aware of the very separate and unequal conditions that exist in the world and in the church. We must force ourselves to take a closer look at the effects our segregationist mentality has had on our present society. Have we indeed left them to huddle together around a pot-bellied stove? Let us go at once into these systems and right our wrongs of the past. God does not love world systems, but he does love the people who are trapped there. Someone must be their champion. Someone who has seen the reality of the Kingdom of God must stand up and proclaim "I have a dream." And then we shall indeed overcome – all of us.

chapter ten

SPIRITUAL FATHERS

Once we decide that we truly are called into this battle for the Kingdom of God, we must approach it as if we are soldiers at war. Every move is critical and we must follow explicitly the commands of our *spiritual fathers* just as a soldier would follow a direct order from his commanding officer.

In order for a young generation to be successful in gaining influence in world systems, they must recognize these spiritual fathers who will offer guidance and direction. The term father or elder usually denotes someone who is older in age. But age is not the only requirement for being a spiritual leader. True spiritual fathers and mothers must be equipped with *sight beyond sight.* They must have the ability to see past the dirt in the field to the possibility of a bountiful harvest. Most of all, these leaders must know how to think strategically and avoid being sedated by the opiate of religious tradition.

These more seasoned men and women of God, who have the ability to see the harvest, *his* harvest, must give wisdom and counsel to a younger generation. An "Esther and Mordecai" relationship must be established between the two for our task to be successful.

I Can See for Miles and Miles

Before the creation of tanks, missiles, aircraft and nuclear weapons, wars were fought by hand to hand combat. The troops would assemble themselves in rank and await the command from the general to attack. In this form of warfare it proved advantageous for the general or commanding officer to sit high up on a hill, so that he could see the entire theatre of battle. From this position he could send in more troops to areas that were short on manpower. He could see when an ambush was coming and alert the troops. It was simply the most efficient place from which to direct the course of battle.

A generation gap of sorts has always existed, I suppose. Younger people, once they have *come of age,* generally view the former generation as out of touch and out of style while they view themselves as the risk takers and the dream makers, the pioneers and the trailblazers who plan to right the wrongs of their parents' generation overnight. Conversely, the generation in power views themselves as the stabilizing force, the backbone of society, the mature, responsible, tax-paying, load bearing citizenry who clean up all the messes and keep the world from falling apart.

The church has not escaped this mentality. The relationship between generations of those called to work for God has slowly deteriorated into one of patronizing and tolerating each other. The blame for this can and must be shared by both parties. I believe the key to reconnecting and reestablishing this vital relationship depends heavily upon the ability of both generations to recognize the importance of the other's gifts and to realize that each must play a different role.

Would Joshua have ever seen the Promised Land and taken the children of Israel there if he had not been willing to sit at the feet of Moses? Younger men and women of God must learn to trust the guidance and judgment of elders in the body of Christ until they, themselves become acquainted with the terms *patience* and *timing!*

Fall Into the Gap

The younger generation must realize that they are not the first to ever hear from God. They must recognize that wisdom is gained from a multitude of counsel. However, wisdom is not gained by listening only to those who always agree with you, nor is it achieved by listening to a multitude of *foolish* counsel. Wise men give wise counsel! And this younger generation must be able to discern by the spirit which elders are truly wise.

Would Joshua have ever seen the promised land and taken the children of Israel there if he had not been willing to sit at the feet of Moses?

*Strategies and
methods are
not absolute,
God's word is
the only
absolute...*

The older generation must recognize that God can and does speak to and through this younger generation. It is critical that both generations be willing to agree that their ultimate goal is the same, reaching the lost. The elders must be open minded enough to realize that successful strategies used in the past may not work in the future. Strategies and methods are not absolute, God's Word is the only absolute, and as long as a particular strategy does not violate that, it should be considered acceptable.

I feel that there is a young generation called out by God who are ready to enter these world systems and strategically gain influence for the Kingdom of God. But everybody knows what can happen if a bunch of immature teenagers are left by themselves for too long and given the freedom to make all their own decisions. In most cases, disaster! In order for our mission to be effective, some generals, elder statesmen in the body of Christ must take their places on the tops of the hills and begin to direct the course of the attack, adding their wisdom and experience to the strength and courage of the young soldiers.

Born in the U.S.A.

When U.S. troops were in Vietnam, they wore camouflage designed to blend in with that environment. It was similar to the jungles and rain forests that typify that region. But years later, when our troops were in the Persian Gulf, the design of the camouflage was changed. Now it had to allow them to blend in with the environment of a desert region.

It would have been idiotic and very dangerous for the Desert Storm Troops to wear the same camouflage as the troops involved in the Vietnam conflict. And even though the United States Armed Forces are unarguably the most powerful in the world, the generals know it would be even more idiotic and dangerous to send troops into any type of covert warfare proudly displaying the red, white and blue of *Old Glory*. If they were going to do that, they might as well mount speakers on their jeeps blaring Bruce Springsteen's *Born in the U.S.A.* during their initial entry into hostile nations. The generals of the U.S. Armed Forces recognize the importance of proper camouflage in battle, and so must the spiritual generals in the body of Christ.

True spiritual generals will see the absolute necessity of allowing the soldiers to enter into world systems undetected and to remain in camouflage until the proper time. The gap between generations in the church will only widen if the older generation attempts to take away the disguise of the younger generation. But it will lessen as the younger generation learns to trust these fathers as they carefully lead them into the *green pastures* of this world, even those that might be considered *no trespassing* zones, as *sheep in wolves' clothing.*

The gap between generations in the church will only widen if the older generation attempts to take away the disguise of the younger generation.

Remember our discussion about natural selection? Our success, and the progeny of generations to follow, rests greatly upon the church's ability to forever close the generation gap. The Promised Land is just over the mountain and God is speaking even now to a generation of Joshua's and Caleb's. God help us not to expend all of our valuable energy fighting each other over what type of music we will or will not allow in church services. Rather let us join forces to fight the *real* battle. It is at hand.

PART FOUR

SECULAR PROPHETS

chapter eleven
UTTERLY ASTOUNDED

chapter twelve
GENERATION X

chapter thirteen
FROM IGNORANCE TO INFLUENCE

finding sacred
in the secular

SECULAR PROPHETS

In Part 3 we talked about the strategy of going out into the world as sheep in wolves' clothing. Now I would like to identify and recognize those sheep who are already in world systems disguised as wolves. Many famous entertainers as well as others who have major influence in the world were born and raised in the house of God. But they were forced into the world by ignorant preachers who incorrectly interpreted scripture into messages of condemnation, making the church nothing but a place of *gloom and doom* for most intelligent, talented people.

Many "ex-churchies" now find themselves in powerful positions in government, the sports world, the academic community, and in business. If the job of the church is to restore, then we must reach out to these people and identify their places of influence, without taking them out of those influential places.

If the job of the church is to restore, then we must reach out to these people and identify their places of influence, without taking them out of those influential places.

**finding sacred
in the secular**

UTTERLY ASTOUNDED

"For the sons of this world are more shrewd in their generation, than the sons of light." These are the words of Jesus found in Luke 16:8. This statement that Jesus made to illustrate a parable haunts me daily, and the reason is this – it seems to become more and more painfully true with every passing day. I watch the sons of this world grow smarter and more shrewd by the hour, while the sons of light remain ignorant and grow more and more out of touch with society.

The sons of this world are constantly acquiring more influence, but for what purpose do they use it? Usually for personal gain and selfish ambition. On the other hand, the sons of light largely have good motives and selfless intentions, but with no influence to wield they are content to hide in the church. They want to help, but can't. The sons of this world can help, but won't. What's wrong with this picture?

In this particular parable (Luke 16), Christ shows how an unjust steward is able to finagle his way out of a situation where he would have lost his position of influence. Christ commends him for being shrewd, even though he was unjustified, and rebukes the sons of light for their inability to act in this manner.

I watch the sons of this world grow smarter and more shrewd by the hour, while the sons of light remain ignorant and grow more and more out of touch with society.

The entire book of Habakkuk, which has never been properly understood by preachers or theologians, is God's attempt to teach the sons of light to be wise and shrewd, like the sons of this world. But only those who have the indwelling power of the Holy Spirit can allow their minds to be open enough to understand the truth contained in this book.

*...sit down,
shut up, and
learn a lesson
from the
Chaldeans!*

In the first chapter, the prophet Habakkuk is crying out to God asking questions regarding the behavior of the Chaldeans. In doing this, what he really wants is for God to sympathize with him and destroy this wicked nation of people. Instead, God basically tells Habakkuk to sit down, shut up, and learn a lesson from the Chaldeans!

God answers Habakkuk's cries by saying, *"Look among the nations and watch — **Be Utterly Astounded!** For I will work a work in your days which you would not believe, though it were told to you! For indeed I am raising up the Chaldeans"* (Habakkuk 1:1-6). And indeed, God did *raise up* the Chaldeans, the *sons of the world* at that time, right before Habakkuk's eyes, and had he watched closely, he would have learned a great lesson from them. In this same way, we, the church can learn lessons today from the sons of this world.

First of all, the Chaldeans *"march through the earth to possess dwelling places that are not theirs."* The sons of this world are not satisfied with their present success, but are ever seeking more success, thus gaining more influence. There is no barrier they will not break through to achieve their desired goal.

Secondly, we see that *"Their horses are swifter than leopards, their chargers charge ahead."* The sons of the world make it their business to be familiar with the latest technology so that they may work very rapidly to accomplish their goal. They do not waste time worrying whether or not the strategy they have chosen to pursue that goal is acceptable to everyone.

Next, we read that *"They all come for violence."* The Kingdom of God suffers violence, and the *violent* take it by force. These worldly people do not take up residence in their comfort zone. Their passion forces them to press on. They exhibit the type of aggressive spirit it takes to gain influence.

Finally, *"They gather captives like sand, they scoff at kings, and princes are scorned by them, they deride every stronghold."* They invade every area of society that may benefit their cause or further their influence. No barrier can withstand the power of their *synergy.* The Chaldeans worked together, like a pack of wolves, to defeat their adversaries. Many times the sons of the world display a greater demonstration of unity in their environment than the body of Christ has ever believed possible. Their unity lies in their commitment to a common goal, not in their agreement on small, miniscule details.

Lead, Follow or
Get Out of the Way

Just as God raised up the Chaldeans and gave them power to gain influence and to deride every stronghold, he is allowing the sons of this world today to surpass what the sons of light are doing. Why? Because the sons of light are either too content or too scared to leave the comfort zone of their four walls, while the sons of this world are bold enough to break through every stronghold and gain influence in this world on a daily basis.

*...the sons of
light are either
too content or
too scared to
leave the
comfort zone
of their four
walls, while
the sons of
this world are
bold enough
to break
through every
stronghold
and gain
influence in
this world on a
daily basis.*

The last part of God's reply to Habakkuk (1:11) says, *"Then his mind changes, and he transgresses; he commits offense, ascribing this power to his god."* God did not consider any of the above mentioned characteristics as offensive or wrong. He meant for Habakkuk to view them as strengths. The only transgression of the Chaldeans that God mentions is when they attributed their victories to themselves or to another god and did not recognize that it was he, Jehovah God who had given them this power to gain influence.

I believe that God is raising up, in this generation, groups of people in the secular world and in secular markets, like the Chaldeans, who are violent in nature and are aggressively deriding every stronghold that would oppose them and their agenda. The church must recognize these people and reach out to them, establish relationships with them and gain their favor. Only then will they accept our instruction and guidance. Only then can we influence them to expand their agendas to include the Kingdom of God!

This may be a good time to rehearse God's first words to Habakkuk: *"Be utterly astounded! For I will work a work in your days which you would not believe, though it were told to you."* Astounded may be a good word to describe how you are feeling right now. Most people, especially Christians, would view the actions and nature of the Chaldeans as destructive and senseless. Again, we must ask God for perspective.

I believe the generation that will see the return of Christ is violent in nature, but not necessarily destructive. They are full of passion but need *spiritual fathers* with perspective and insight to help *harness* and *direct* their passion for the Kingdom of God. I believe the body of Christ has transgressed regarding this generation. We have cursed this generation and ascribed their behavior to another god, the god of this world, Satan. We have transgressed because we have written them off as a violent generation and have prayed for God to deal with them as He dealt with Sodom and Gomorrah. We have believed that the best we can hope for is that God would destroy them and start with a new generation. Again, I say we have transgressed!

God has given these characteristics to this generation in order to establish His Kingdom on the earth. Regaining the influence and authority that Satan has stolen will take a violent and aggressive generation who can, like the Chaldeans, deride every stronghold of Satan.

*We cannot
continue to
pray against
the very
attributes that
they must
possess to
usher in the
Kingdom of
God!*

We must realize that this is the *last* generation. We cannot continue to pray against the very attributes that they must possess to usher in the Kingdom of God! God has given them a passionate nature for such a time as this. We must cease from our efforts to *change* them and find ways to *channel* them!

Fight the Power

Consider for a moment Benjamin Franklin's incredible gift of perspective. While everyone who surrounds him runs for shelter, fearful of this dreaded thing called lightning, he flies a kite. Why is he flying a kite in a lightning storm? This man must be crazy! Right? Or does he have the ability to see potential that others do not? Others ignorantly curse these loud, bright bolts of light because they do not comprehend the possibility of their power.

Benjamin Franklin believed that if he could only *harness* this energy, he could channel it positively to perform incredible tasks. And today we all enjoy the results of his ability to do just that. Imagine the ridicule and shame that came his way until his experiments proved successful. Also imagine all we would have missed if this one man had not seen with perspective and had not persevered through the mocking and disbelief to complete his mission.

Dream with me for a moment of the possibilities for the Kingdom of God if we could positively harness this generation's passion and violent energy. The problem is not their violent nature. The only problem is that they are using this energy for the wrong kingdom. Energy not properly channeled becomes an explosion. The church's problem is that we have tried to change and subdue this God-given passion rather than channel it.

The church's problem is that we have tried to change and subdue this God-given passion rather than channel it.

It is interesting to note that the kite Franklin flew had a *key* attached to it. The *key* to harnessing the energy of this generation rests in the response of spiritual fathers and mothers. The future of this violent generation depends on the church's willingness to get out in the storm and get our kites up in the air. Is it worth the risk? I say yes. It's time to stop *fighting their power* – we're not winning. We must embrace it, seek

to understand it, harness it, and then stand trium-
phantly atop it and guide it home – back home to
God's Kingdom.

chapter twelve

GENERATION X

Sometime around 1989 or 1990, some incredibly small-minded writer labeled a whole generation of young people as simply "X". The "X" supposedly means that there is no significant attribute to typify or describe them. Reporters and journalists jumped on the bandwagon and began to instill fear in the minds of an older generation that the generation coming behind them would utterly fail when given the responsibility of running this country.

Although this "X" may be the label they carry, it is ridiculous to suggest that there are no outstanding characteristics belonging to this generation. They may not always make the best decisions, but they are certainly not void of passion. Those Christians who curse this generation for its violent and passionate spirit need to realize that violence is not the worst attribute a generation can possess, apathy is. At least violence is a form of energy, and as discussed, can be harnessed or channeled. Apathy is a lack of energy and a desire for nothing. You can not positively channel energy that does not exist. I believe God has his hand upon this violent generation and has purposed for them to manifest his kingdom here on earth.

...violence is not the worst attribute a generation can possess, apathy is.

'Dem Bones

In order to avoid becoming corny or too cliche I will not refer to them as Generation "Next," Generation "X-Cited," Generation "X-it" (exit), Generation "X-ample", etc. Using these phrases usually turns people of true passion and vision off. So how do we describe this generation? While taking a class on the Major Prophets of the Old Testament I came across the book of Ezekiel. When I began to study the 37th chapter of this book, I felt the Holy Spirit speaking to me concerning this generation. Ezekiel 37:1-14 is the vision of the *dry bones* that God gave to Ezekiel. As I read this story I began to realize that this generation is similar to these bones, waiting only for the prophet to speak the word of life over them.

In the first two verses we see the Spirit of God bringing Ezekiel to the valley and causing him to pass by and notice these bones. He literally forces Ezekiel to go and sit in this valley of desolation! Evidence of the Holy Spirit in our lives is more than the gibberish of an unknown language; it is our ability to see the pain and hurts of those who surround us.

In verse 3 God asks Ezekiel a very crucial question, "Can these bones live?" This question is the pivotal element in this story. In my estimation an omniscient

God does not ask questions because He does not know the answers. He does not pose this question to Ezekiel to see if the prophet can give him some new insight or knowledge on the matter. God is fixing Ezekiel's perception of these bones! The future of this multitude of dry and lifeless bones depends on Ezekiel's perception of what they can become, not on their present state. When God asked Ezekiel, *"Son of man, can these bones live?"* he wanted to know what Ezekiel saw — a valley of dry, lifeless and hopeless bones? Or the potential for a mighty army?

...the future of this genera- tion lies in our perception of what they can be, not what they are right now.

In the following verses the prophet speaks life and structure to these bones and they begin to come together. What words do we speak over this generation called "X"? Do we see the potential for a mighty army or a hopeless pile of bones? *"Out of the abundance of the heart, the mouth speaks."* Sometimes we forget that the power of life and death is in our tongue. Like the bones, the future of this generation lies in our perception of what they can be, not what they are right now. How can they become a mighty army for God when we see only dry bones? How can they be full of life when we continually speak death over them?

The Answer My Friend is Blowin' in the Wind

An interesting characteristic of the army God is form-ing today is its diversity. In Ezekiel 37:9 the life that the Spirit of God is blowing into this lifeless body is described as coming from the *four winds.* The Spirit of God that will blow into this generation is indeed coming from the four corners of the earth, and is trans-mitting a spirit of understanding and acceptance of different cultures into it. Unlike God's remnant from the past, this army is not so nationalistic and exclu-sive that they lack world-vision. They are diverse in their backgrounds and knowledgeable of the customs and beliefs of cultures other than their own. The Spirit of God coming from the four winds will literally blow a trans-cultural nature into this army.

They will have the inherent ability to fulfill the scrip-ture in Matthew 24:14 *"and this gospel of the king-dom will be preached into all the world as a witness to all nations, and then the end will come."* In order for this gospel not only to be preached, but to be preached as a *witness* to all nations, we must know enough about the particular culture of each of those nations to be able to relate it to them in a way they can understand it and accept it as truth.

Beauty is in the Eye
of the Beholder

"The lamp of the body is the eye. If therefore your eye is good, your whole body will be full of light. But if your eye is bad, your whole body will be full of darkness" (Matthew 6:22,23). Because Ezekiel's *eye was good,* because he perceived that these dry bones could be a great army, they were. When he sees them in verse 10, standing as *an exceedingly great army,* the Spirit of God then says to Ezekiel that *"these bones are the whole house of Israel."*

The army of God in these last days will be comprised largely of those who at one time were disillusioned with the church because of its inability to relate truth in a spirit of love. Its soldiers will be those young people who were almost lost from the Kingdom of God because of hireling preachers and false prophets who did not speak the words of life over them.

The dry bones in the book of Ezekiel were the bones of people who had said of themselves *"our hope is lost, and we ourselves are cut off!"* However, there was a prophet who was used by God to restore life and purpose to them because his vision was not limited to their present state of being. Ezekiel saw through the eyes of the Spirit of God what these dry bones could be.

How many hundreds of thousands, if not millions, of young people are there out there today who grew up in church but now find themselves feeling hopeless, lost and cut off from God? They are our sons, our daughters, our brothers, our sisters, our cousins, our nieces and nephews, our grandchildren, our friends. These are the dry bones of the house of Israel, waiting for someone to breathe the power of the Holy Spirit into them.

What will become of this generation if we do not pray for the spirit and insight of Ezekiel to fall upon the church? What will become of our disillusioned sons and daughters? Will they remain as dry, lifeless, hopeless, dead bones? Or will they rise as did the bones in the book of Ezekiel and be brought back into the house of God? We must begin to pray that God would give his appointed and anointed prophets the ability to *speak things that are not as though they were* so that we may answer the question the Holy Spirit asks us today: *"Son of man, can these bones live?"*

FROM IGNORANCE
TO INFLUENCE

The words of the screaming preacher rang out: "Do you not know that the unrighteous will not inherit the Kingdom of God? Do not be deceived. Neither fornicators, nor idolaters, nor adulterers, nor homosexuals, nor sodomites, nor thieves, nor covetous, nor drunkards, nor revilers, nor extortioners will inherit the Kingdom of God." His words shook the walls of the small holiness church, frightening the children. For all his seeming zeal, this red-faced little man totally misses the crux of the message of this scripture when he omits the very next verse . . . "And such were some of y**ou.**"

You Push Me Away

Young men and women in churches like this all across this country have never had the opportunity to hear that verse that says, *"But you were washed, but you were sanctified, but you were justified in the name of the Lord Jesus and by the Spirit of our God."* Therefore, they left! They have never heard of a merciful God who stands eagerly waiting to forgive them if they will only ask. Their last memory of church is the sight of an angry little man, vehemently spewing condemnation and guilt from his mouth. Tragically, many formed their concept of God based on this memory. I serve a God who is so awesome that he uses the angry words of an ignorant preacher to serve his own purposes and to advance his ultimate plan. Thus, even the fire and brimstone condemnation message can be viewed as strategic. Why? Because its words of condemnation and judgment forced many people out of the church and into the world. God knew that his eternal Kingdom would never be manifested here on earth as long as we, the church, were content to hide inside its four walls. So even the words of an ignorant preacher must be viewed as extremely necessary for these end times.

Those who have been disillusioned by religious bondage and condemnation preaching are now exactly where God needs them, in the world.

Many who left were able to gain influence with the "unsaved" because they did not scare them away with the same religious attitude that had once scared them away. The ignorance of the church has forced many people born in the church to act shrewdly, like the sons of the world, without even knowing it! Those who have been disillusioned by religious bondage and condemnation preaching are now exactly where God needs them, in the world.

Tell Me Something Good

It seems as if God knew what he was doing all the time. When the church began to preach the come out from among them and be separate message, it made us inaccessible to the world, the people God loves and gave Himself for. So God had to change strategies. He began to raise a generation who would not tolerate ignorance and exclusivism. He knew that the church's ignorance would force them into the world where they would be able to gain influence. Now is the time to begin to recognize who these people are and present them with the gospel of good news: The gospel of grace.

Many of these lost sheep are actually not lost. They are exactly where the Good Shepherd wants them and needs them, in the greenest pastures of world systems. Many famous musicians and entertainers who top the musical charts today began their singing careers in church. Somewhere in their childhood they were turned off to church because they were exposed to religious hypocrisy and condemnation. But they were never turned off to Jesus. Just watch any of the major awards shows and you will hear performer after performer thank or at least acknowledge God.

When we begin to realize that these influential people would be very receptive to a gospel of good news rather than legalism we will gain their attention. Once spiritual fathers take the initiative to form relationships of acceptance with these people, we can finally put down our fishing poles and pick up the dragnet.

Many of these lost sheep are actually not lost. They are exactly where the Good Shepherd wants them and needs them, in the greenest pastures of world systems.

Once spiritual fathers take the initiative to form relationships of acceptance with these people, we can finally put down our fishing poles and pick up the dragnet.

*Many church
leaders do not
understand
the strategy of
using influen-
tial people in
influential
places.*

*But these
relationships
will never be
effective if
their spiritual
father seeks to
remove them
from their
place of
influence.*

In 1993, I was in charge of coordinating a youth conference for the young people in my church. The musical group that was featured drew about 2,500 young people to our conference. As I watched the young people walk into the building I was overwhelmed with joy and thankfulness. To say the least I felt like I had accomplished something. When I came home that evening I flipped on the television. What I saw brought me a feeling of correction and frustration. Pearl Jam, who was a very popular rock group in the early 90's and is still on the top of the charts, was doing an outdoor concert. As the camera panned the audience I was astounded at the number of young people I saw. I estimated at least a quarter of a million. The announcer later said that the final count was over three quarters of a million people. I realized at that moment that I was still fishing with a rod and reel. I promised myself that day that I would not rest until I was serving the Kingdom of God by utilizing the strategy of the dragnet.

Many leaders in the church do not understand the strategy of utilizing influential people in influential places. This is why they are satisfied with having several thousand young people at conferences, rather than several million. The relationships we as Christians create with these people of influence could be used to bring incredible influence to the Kingdom of God. But these relationships will never be effective if their spiritual father seeks to remove them from their place of influence.

$$ It's All About the Benjamins $$

I had the opportunity to attend a musical concert several years ago that changed my life. The young man, and multi-millionaire, who was producing and performing in the show is known as Sean "Puffy" Combs or "Puff Daddy" or "Puffy." At the end of this evening of loud and aggressive music and rap, he stopped the entire act. A gospel choir came onto the stage and began to sing worship choruses. "Puffy" then began to literally lead these thousands of unsaved kids into worship!

Immediately my skeptical mind began to work. I said to myself, "It's popular these days to give God glory at awards banquets. How is this any different?" Then he stopped the choir and said, "I know many of you may think that I am being a hypocrite." You may ask, "How can he do the things on stage that he does and then talk about how much he loves God? First I had to relate with you where you are. If I came up here from the beginning talking about Jesus and loving the Lord you would have either walked out or booed me off the stage. But, I got you here didn't I?"

At that moment, I saw more of the nature and character of Christ displayed on the stage that night than I had seen in a long time! Christ became a man, human flesh, mortal. In Jesus, divinity meets humanity, and just as Christ became like us in order to save us, this young rap artist met the unsaved that night right where they were for the purpose of sharing the gospel.

I'm sure that more than one pastor has preached against people like this young man and has discouraged the teenagers in his church from listening to music like his. What a shame. The influence he has already gained in the world of entertainment is priceless. The time has come for Spiritual Mordecai's to begin to trust some modern day Esther's and work together to reap an incredibly bountiful harvest.

Another One Bites the Dust

We take them (famous people) out of their natural environment and put them in our trophy case for all to see.

The problem with this strategy is that pastors are so eager to have famous people in their churches that when someone from the entertainment world gives their life to Christ we want to monopolize and control their time and their gift from then on. We expect them to change the very things about themselves that drew others to them and made them famous to begin with. We take them out of their natural environment and put them in our trophy case for all to see. It seems almost as if we are hunting wild animals to shoot and mount on our walls. A deer does not belong in a pastor's office. It belongs in its natural habitat. Although it feels like we are protecting them, we are actually making them more vulnerable to emotional and spiritual disaster when we take these people out of the place where they are comfortable; out of the place where they have worked so hard to gain influence; and confine them only to the church world, which they know little or nothing about.

The Spiritual Mordecai's of the church must remember that God has strategically placed them where they are for a reason—to gain influence. This green pasture known to us as world systems is the very place where these people thrive. It is their natural habitat. But in a moment of pride, we take away years of God's process of helping these people gain influence.

This green pasture, known to us as world systems, is the very place where these people thrive - it is their natural habitat.

Places Everyone!

I pray that God would begin to raise a generation of Kingdom Generals — Spiritual Fathers who know how to stay where they are supposed to stay – up on top of the hill directing the course of battle. The general does not run down the mountain every thirty minutes to look over the soldier's shoulder or to "do lunch" with him. He stays on the hill, close enough to God to hear his voice and know his direction, and high enough to see with proper perspective both the possibility of ambush and the door of opportunity. And although this is his assigned position, and the vantage point from where he is most effective, it is not that of the soldiers. He does not invite the soldiers up the hill to fraternize. They are needed on the front line. And as they are there, risking their lives in battle, he is in his place on the hill to guide, direct, advise and to raise the battle cry, "Yes, there are giants to face, but greater is he that is in us than he that is in the world!"

PART FIVE

THE NEW SOUND

chapter fourteen
BY ANY MEANS NECESSARY

chapter fifteen
CHANGING OF
THE LEVITICAL ORDER

chapter sixteen
THE NEW SOUND

finding sacred
in the secular

BY ANY MEANS NECESSARY

The South of the 1960's can be variously categorized. Segregationists would say this was a tragic time for our country and the beginning of the demise of our nation. Others would say it was a time of needless violence. Still others would classify this time as a move of God.

One man stands out to those familiar with the Civil Rights Movement, Dr. Martin Luther King, Jr. His strategy of non-violence proved to be a way for the African-American voice to be heard in this nation. A strategy not as threatening as some of the tactics of groups such as the Black Panther's or of people such as Malcolm X.

Ain't That Peculiar

For some reason most white Americans remember Dr. King as a respectable and intelligent man. They do not view him as a violent or threatening individual. However, some of the same people who eagerly celebrate the national holiday in Dr. King's honor are disgusted and terrified at the image and remembrance of Malcolm X.

These people never understood the Civil Rights Movement and will probably not understand this book. The same people who feel outrage over Malcolm X would pat Dr. King on the back and say, "I like you! You're not like the rest of them." Ignorantly, these people do not realize that Dr. King must have felt, at some time, the same emotions of anger as Malcolm X. He just expressed his anger differently.

Malcolm X was not an evil man, but a man who had grown tired of seeing his loved ones abused and mistreated. His response was not evil or even abnormal. His response was as normal as protecting your family from a burglar who has broken into your house. What most Americans miss is that Dr. King's response was extremely *abnormal*.

Be Ye Angry and Sin Not

What kind of man can control his anger when someone is spitting in his face or washing his wife down the street with a fire hose? The kind of man who knew he was out-numbered and out-matched. The kind of man who was smart enough to realize that a violent response would only lead to more bloodshed. The kind of man who had enough insight to understand it was not violence that would cause the rest of the nation to see the atrocities taking place in the South. He knew that the nation would only be more incensed if the "colored" folk fought back. He knew that they would be more sympathetic if they saw the black community suffer the abuse without retaliation. Dr. Martin Luther King, Jr. should be remembered as an incredibly intelligent and strategic man. However, he should not be remembered as a man who felt no anger.

The anger that he and every other African-American felt was expressed through the uncontrolled outbursts of emotion from Malcolm X. I can honestly say that if my family had been treated the way most southern African-American families were treated in the 1960's my natural response would not have been facilitated through non-violent means. *Passive resistance* would definitely not have been my first thought. If I had been an African-American man at that time I probably would have responded much more like Malcolm X did: "Let's kick some ass."

Although Malcolm X is remembered as a great leader in the African-American community, he did not succeed in changing one piece of legislation that concerned the advancement of black people in a white society. He was successful in showing the white man that he was upset, but laws such as the Equal Employment Act and the right for African-Americans to vote must be attributed to Dr. King's crusade.

In the same way that we remember Dr. King for his *I Have A Dream* speech, we remember Malcolm X for the encapsulating statement of his philosophy, *By Any*

143

Means Necessary. This statement proposes the idea that if freedom cannot be gained through *passive resistance* then it must be gained through violence. The thinking behind this statement represents years of abuse and neglect that ultimately surfaced in reckless abandonment.

Different Strokes

To change perspectives for a moment, this statement can actually be compared to Paul's writings in I Corinthians. The ninth chapter of this letter speaks of the Apostle's desire to reach different types of people from different walks of life. The strategy he gives is to relate to them by means of their own particular culture. He concludes the letter by saying, *"I have become all things to all men, that I might by all means save some. Now this I do for the gospel's sake..."*

The time has come for the body of Christ to adopt the *By Any Means Necessary* theory. We must again become relevant to this sinful world that Christ loves and died for so that we might *by all means* save some. Many in the church have already adopted this theory in word but we have failed to implement it through our deeds.

Our response is similar to that of Malcolm X. We have become fed up with the way Satan has kept us in bondage for years and we have let him know that we are upset. We have stomped on him during church services. We have rebuked him and cast him out. We have called him a plethora of derogatory names. Yet, we still have not changed anything. If we are truly fed up with the attacks of Satan against the body of Christ we have got to do more than let him know that we are angry. We must do more than sit in church Sunday after Sunday commiserating with each other about how badly Satan has treated us. We must do more than threaten. We must take action. We must *change some legislation.*

How do we change legislation? How do we actually do something about the condition of this world that God loves and that Satan has tried to destroy? As has been stated over and over in this book, we have got to go into his territory.

The hardest blow we can inflict upon Satan is to steal back from him the authority he has taken from the Kingdom of God and locked away in world systems. But this will never happen as long as we continue to act on our emotions. Our feelings of anger toward his work on the earth are right and proper. However, it has only been expressed in word. Threatening screams from our pulpits must be facilitated through our ability to sneak behind enemy lines and rescue hostages.

We have stomped on Satan during church services - we have rebuked him and cast him out. We have called him a plethora of derogatory names. Yet, we still have not changed anything.

Threatening screams from the pulpit must be facilitated through our ability to sneak behind enemy lines and rescue hostages.

J-J-J Jive Talkin'

When I was growing up my father always told me not to say things that I could not back up. In athletic arenas there is a phenomenon known as *trash talking*. *Trash talking* is done by a player on one team to a player on the opposing team. The purpose of this is to intimidate and distract your opponent and to take him *out of his game*. Ironically, I have been on the other end of some serious *trash talking* done by players who were not good enough to be the water boy. I have played in basketball games where I have scored more than forty points against my opponent only to continually hear him in my ear talk about how awesome he is and how awful I am.

In some respects this is the way we sound in the ear of Satan. He is literally embarrassing us to the point where we should not be allowed back on the court. He is continuously winning the game and scoring an outrageous number of points. However, we are still *trash talking* and acting as if we are winning. Imagine if Howard Stern and Michael Jordan were to play one on one. Sure, Howard Stern would win the *talking game,* but in reality Michael Jordan would destroy him.

Our attempts to scare Satan have not worked. We have not talked him out if his game plan or intimidated him. We have become like a little dog chasing a train. He may bark really loudly, but the train continues to roll on. The only way we can win is to derail the train. We have got to go a few miles ahead of the train and set up a roadblock or even better, an explosion. The only way that we win is by making this earth the footstool of God. This can be done by returning the lost influence of the Kingdom of God back to God the Father. This lost influence can be retrieved only by a strategic infiltration of world systems and secular society!

The only way that we can win is by making this earth the footstool of God. This can be done by returning the lost influence of the Kingdom of God back to God the Father.

finding sacred
in the secular

CHANGING THE LEVITICAL ORDER

In order for us to successfully retrieve this lost authority and influence, and to return all power and authority back to God there must be a radical change in our methodology. As God's appointed leaders and shepherds we must take another look at our approach and at our game plan. The Levitical Order is simply an Old Testament term used to refer to the group of priests and elders who ministered in the temple. It began with the tribe of Levi, or Levites as they were called, who were the original priesthood. Any reference the house of Levi is suggestive of an anointing of God to minister or be a priest that is passed down from generation to generation through the bloodline.

I believe there must be a complete paradigm shift in the way the church views its pastors and in the way they view themselves. The modern day pastor's job description needs nothing less than a revolution in order to be truly effective. The paradigm of a pastor sitting by the phone eagerly awaiting an opportunity to counsel someone must change. The truth is most counseling sessions could be avoided if people would seek first the Kingdom of God and truly find their purpose. Happiness does not come from sitting in coun-

The modern day Pastor's job description needs nothing less than a revolution in order to be truly effective.

seling sessions. Happiness comes from being in the will of God and from knowing that you are helping to establish his Kingdom on earth.

Even though I have been in the ministry only a few years, I have already spent hours counseling women whose biggest problem is that they are unhappy because their husbands want to watch television during dinner. After listening to them talk for these hours I can truly say I'm not surprised that their husbands prefer to watch T.V. Maybe for some pastors this type of counseling is fulfilling. Not for me!

Time after time I have emphasized in this book that the Kingdom of God suffers violence and the violent take it by force. I mentioned in the beginning of the book that I believe a violent spirit has been birthed in me, and ever since then I seem to want nothing but to find new ways of gaining influence in world systems. Somehow I believe my time can be better spent for God's Kingdom than sitting in my office listening to people belly-ache.

Pastors of the new millennium should not limit their studies to theology and seminary work.

Wouldn't It Be Nice?

The pastor of the future must be able to lead his sheep into green pastures. If this is to be so, it will be necessary for him to be aware of where these places of influence are and be familiar enough with them to lead others down the path. Pastors of the new millennium should not limit their studies to theology and seminary work. They should also be knowledgeable in the law, government, entertainment, education, science, medicine, etc.

The *counseling session* of the future must become more than a place for people to vent all their negative emotions to someone who they know will just say, "There, there – I'll agree in prayer with you about that," and not be honest enough to tell them the truth. No longer should there be lengthy counseling sessions that must be followed up with more counseling and sessions, week after week after week. Time spent between pastors and parishioners should be given mostly to strategic planning of their lives and what their role in God's ultimate plan is.

Wouldn't it be wonderful if pastors spent all their time discussing with their people the next area of government they are going to invade, the next airline they are going to take over, the next television station they are going to buy, the next movie they are going to make? Now we are talking about a paradigm shift. Wouldn't it be more exciting to talk about what new nation we are going to run than what color the new choir robes should be?

*As long as the
body of Christ
is more
excited about
seeing a
miracle than
gaining
influence in
world sys-
tems, his
Kingdom will
never come.
And Christ will
continue to be
held in the
heavens until
we do our
part.*

Don't You Cry No More

There are just too many *sucklings* in our churches who have been Christians for years yet still need to suck on the pastor's breast. *"By this time you ought to be teachers."* All of the blame for this situation cannot be attributed to the laity of the church. In fact, most of the responsibility for this co-dependent relationship belongs squarely on the pastors' shoulders. Pastors must learn to wean the *sucklings* by giving them purpose. We need to hear more messages from pulpits that leave parishioners feeling like they have a job to do. Then, *counseling sessions* can be turned into *strategy sessions.*

Many times we create the atmosphere for this *suckling* mentality without even realizing it. As long as the body of Christ is more excited about seeing a miracle than gaining influence in world systems, his Kingdom will never come, and Christ will continue to be held in the heavens until we do our part.

Jesus said, *"It is an adulterous generation that seeks a sign."* We have encouraged people to seek signs rather than sound doctrine. Our itching ears have caused us to turn away from truth and listen to fables, frankly because most of the time they are more *excit-ing.* When people are no longer willing to endure sound doctrine we give them what they want – a show – a sign. But miracles do not establish the Kingdom of God, gaining influence does.

The Bible says that signs, wonders and miracles will follow those who believe. Did you catch the order of that sentence? *They* follow *us*! We don't follow them. *Side-show* church services must stop. It's time for *those who believe* to stop running from church to church, auditorium to auditorium champing at the bit to see someone *fall out* or laugh uncontrollably or be frozen in some strange position for hours. Let's go out into the world and let the signs and wonders and follow us *there*. Now that would really be a *miracle*! And that's where miracles are most effective anyway, where the people are who don't believe — not in the church where people are already believers.

Wanna Be Startin' Something

A key strategy in this next millennium will indeed include those who have been anointed by God for the explicit purpose of going out into the secular world and becoming successful. But, as we send these *Esther's* into the palace, our role as *Mordecai* is going to be increasingly more important. Mordecai must direct the next generation as they set up and develop their *ministries* in secular markets.

153

*I believe that
God is going
to anoint a
select few to
pastor from a
different type
of office.
These new
offices will
include
recording
studios
(secular),
movie sets,
offices of
government,
etc.*

The pastor of the future will not necessarily perform his ministry from behind a pulpit. I believe that will always be necessary. However, I also believe that the definition of what an *effective* pastor is can no longer be limited and confined to preaching, counseling and administrating a church. I believe that God is going to anoint a select few to pastor from a different type of office. These new offices will include recording studios (secular), movie sets, offices of government, etc. Under God's anointing, a remnant will be lead into the secular markets of our day to gain influence.

I recently read a prophecy that Rick Joyner gave to the body of Christ in the late eighties. He explained how God was going to anoint *cross-over* artists in the secular world for the purpose of reaping an incredible harvest. His exact words were, "The Lord is going to anoint some of His minstrels with a new sound that will capture men's attention and sow the seeds of the gospel in their hearts, without ever mentioning the Lord or sounding like religious music... It is important for these minstrels not to look religious or talk 'religioneze.'" That time is now! *"Do not say there are four months and then comes the harvest, but behold, I say unto you, lift up your eyes for the hour is now."*

THE NEW SOUND

I am a dog lover and own two Old English Mastiffs. For those of you who don't know, the Mastiff is the largest breed of dog in the world. My male, Duke, weighs 240 pounds and is taller than I am when he stands on his hind legs. If you have ever spent any time around dogs you know that their hearing is extremely sensitive. Just listen to the dogs in your neighborhood howl the next time any vehicle with a loud siren drives through.

When I was growing up, my father bred and showed Doberman Pinschers. He trained them with a dog whistle. I was always fascinated as a child when he would put it to his lips and blow. Although Dad and I couldn't hear a thing, the dogs would immediately respond because they have the ability to hear on a higher frequency than humans do.

Tune In and Turn On

Similarly, I believe that God speaks on a wavelength or frequency that many people are unable to tune in to. And I believe that God is beginning to emit a sound throughout the earth that only certain people will hear. This *new sound* will be heard only by those who have the ability to tap into this frequency.

...I believe that God is beginning to emit a sound throughout the earth that only certain people will hear.

Revelation 14 speaks of a generation to come who will hear this new sound. It says that these people will hear a sound and sing a song that others are unable to. Don't confuse me with a Jehovah's Witness. I don't believe that there are only 144,000 who are redeemed, but I do believe that there is a chosen group or a remnant who will be able to hear the sound of these new, non-traditional strategies God is sending out on his frequency.

Not everyone will be able to hear the *sound* that tells them to infiltrate secular music as sheep in wolves' clothing. All of God's people will not understand the *sound* of reaching out to the homosexual community without condemnation or judgmentalism. The idea that God is moving more in secular markets through people who have gained influence there than he is in the church will not be believed and accepted by all believers, because they cannot hear on that frequency.

These people who will hear this new sound will be able to do so because they have not been corrupted by or touched with the filth of religiosity.

Like A Virgin

This chapter in Revelation goes on to describe this chosen group of people as *virgins*. I don't think he's talking in the natural realm about physical virgins, but rather *spiritual* virgins. These people who will hear this new sound will be able to do so because they have not been corrupted by or touched with the filth of religiosity. They are naïve and ignorant of the fact that all Christians are supposed to build up barriers between themselves and the world. God has literally chosen to put a spiritual *chastity belt* around their minds so that they are not impregnated with the traditions of religion and can remain in tune with the groans of secular society.

John also describes these people as *faultless.* He says there is no *"deceit found in their mouths."* They are still human, so are obviously not without sin. So what does this mean? I think it means that they are so aware of their own fleshly weaknesses that they dare not speak a word of judgment to anyone else. Therefore, there is no dissension among the brethren, the thing that God hates most.

The last part of this chapter says that they are first fruits among many brethren and that they follow the lamb wherever he goes. This includes following Jesus into the places where hurting people are held captive in world systems.

Are You Gonna' Go My Way?

Jesus sits at the right hand of God the Father waiting for this earth to again be made his footstool. He waits for all authority and power to be given back to God. He waits for us, his bride, to reclaim all of the influence and power that Satan has had locked away in world systems since his rebellion and fall.

I long to be with Jesus. I long to live in a new heaven and a new earth. I long to see every knee bow before his throne and to hear every tongue confess that Jesus Christ is Lord. So let's get busy making this earth His footstool! Can you hear the sound?

Then the seventh angel sounded: And there were loud voices in heaven, saying, "The kingdoms of this world have become the kingdoms of our Lord and of His Christ, and He shall reign forever and ever!"

finding sacred
in the secular

**the
new sound**

finding sacred
in the secular